# Sister Germana's
# ITALIAN
# COOKBOOK

# Sister Germana's
# ITALIAN
# COOKBOOK

**THE BEST IN ITALIAN CUISINE
FEATURING EASY-TO-MAKE DISHES
OF HEALTHFUL AND DELICIOUS FOODS
FOR EVERY OCCASION**

**Illustrated**

CATHOLIC BOOK PUBLISHING CO.
NEW YORK

This book was originally published in Italian under the title *Quando Cucinano gli Angeli!* by Edizioni Piemme, Casale Monferrato. The English translation was made by Annemarie Mazzella.

(T-178)

# CONTENTS

## PART ONE

5

8                            CONTENTS

# CONTENTS

# PREFACE

I HAVE written this book for at least 10 "reasons," spontaneously and enthusiastically, knowing that I am helping many friends and all those people who will be able to use it.

Here are my "ten commandments" that tell why I have written this book.

1. I believe in the value of good cooking as an occasion to help people smile and feel loved.

2. Every dish can become a manifestation of attention, a statement that it is beautiful to be together at this important time of the day.

3. The preparation of good food is a language understood by all.

4. I have worked so hard to learn to cook in a simple and efficient way that I want to spare others the fear of failure.

5. I want to make available to others 20 years of experience in avoiding failures and frustrations.

6. The heart is close to the stomach.

7. Good health and good cooking make life more livable.

8. When I go home my mother regularly prepares for me the things that I prefer and in this way proves that she knows my tastes and loves me.

9. When people enter the kitchen as I am cooking, they all stop and forget where they were going.

10. When I serve a meal people light up as if they had not eaten for a week.

Around the table the quiet become talkative. Everyone gets along. . . . It is fun and moving at the same time. I understand why Christ chose mealtime to do the beautiful things he did. He understood and encouraged people.

# PART ONE

# 1

## WHEN YOUR WIFE IS AT THE SHORE

*If you're lucky and have an ideal wife, together you agree on vacation dates, decide when your wife and children will depart and on the length of their stay. If that's the case, certainly your wife, knowing your tastes and your ability in the kitchen, will do the shopping and leave in the house all that you'll need. She'll buy the nonperishables and leave to you only the daily or weekly shopping for milk, bread, vegetables and fruit, meat and fresh cheese. In the refrigerator she will have for you: butter, eggs, Parmesan cheese, salami, some potatoes, seasonings, onions, tomatoes. Lemons, oil, vinegar, pasta, rice, canned tomatoes, some tuna, anchovies, sardines, capers, etc., will also be on hand.*

*If, then, you are very lucky and have a wife who loves you and good cooking, she will leave the freezer full of prepared dishes with instructions on how to cook them, when to take them out of the freezer, etc. Then life is simple and beautiful.*

*If you have to see to everything but have the major groceries in the house, don't be alarmed. I'll give you some ideas. If you have nothing in the house, read above what your wife should have bought, buy it yourself, and with the joy of one who is capable of taking care of himself read on and do.*

★    ★    ★

### SPAGHETTI, TOMATOES, BASIL, GARLIC, AND OIL

*Ingredients for 2 servings:*

6  oz. spaghetti
2  sprigs basil
2  medium-sized ripe tomatoes
2  tablespoons oil
2  cloves garlic

In a saucepan with 1 quart of water, add 1 teaspoon of salt and bring to a boil.

When the water boils add 2 tablespoons of oil (which prevents the spaghetti from sticking together). Add the spaghetti stirring well. Follow the package directions for cooking time. While the pasta is cooking, wash the tomatoes and basil. Mince the tomatoes and basil separately.

In a small pan with 2 tablespoons of oil, brown the garlic. Strain the pasta, put it in a bowl, add the minced tomato, and mix well. Add the minced basil and pour the boiling oil and garlic over all. Mix and serve.

● This is an excellent dish because the tomatoes and basil remain raw retaining their important vitamins.

## RICE WITH CHEESE

*Ingredients for 2 servings:*

**4 oz. good quality rice**
**1 oz. fontina cheese, cubed**
**1 oz. Swiss cheese, cubed**
**1 oz. mozzarella cheese, cubed**
**2 tablespoons Parmesan cheese**
**2 tablespoons extra virgin-olive oil**

Heat a quart of water, to which has been added 1 teaspoon of salt, to boiling. When the water boils add the rice, stir, and let it cook uncovered for 15 minutes.

Drain the rice and return it to the pot, adding the cubed cheese and the oil. Heat over a low flame just until the cheese melts. Add the Parmesan and serve.

● This can be a meal in itself (it's nourishing). All you need to complete it is a tossed salad or fruit salad.

★          ★          ★

## NOODLES WITH BUTTER AND SAGE

*Ingredients for 2 servings:*

8 oz. fresh noodles
or
6 oz. dried noodles
1 oz. (2 tablespoons) butter
4 leaves sage
Parmesan cheese

Put 1 tablespoon of salt in a quart of water and heat to boiling. Add the pasta, stirring so the noodles don't stick together. Cook fresh noodles for 5 minutes; if dried noodles are used cook for 10 minutes. When the pasta is cooking, brown the butter and sage in a pan over low heat.

Drain the pasta returning it to the pot, add the butter and sage, add the Parmesan. Mix and serve.

• This dish is simply delicious and also healthy because sage is rich in healthy benefits. It is calming, refreshing, and digestible.

## GNOCCHI WITH GORGONZOLA CHEESE

*Ingredients for 2 servings:*

6 oz. gnocchi
4 on. gorgonzola cheese
1 oz. (2 tablespoons) butter
1 tablespoon Parmesan cheese

Bring to a boil a quart of salted (1 teaspoon) water. Throw in the gnocchi. Usually, Sardinian gnocchi are made of durum wheat and don't cook in less than 20 minutes. They take well to boiling. (They have more patience to wait than the others!)

While the pasta is cooking cut the gorgonzola cheese into pieces. In a large pan heat the butter and the cut gorgonzola. You'll see that the cheese will melt.

Now drain the pasta and put it in the pan together with the gorgonzola. Mix it all together and heat through. Add the Parmesan cheese and eat this hearty dish!

• In this case you can eat just a tossed salad and nothing else. Remember you have just eaten pasta and cheese. All you need to add are vitamins and minerals.

★        ★        ★

## SPAGHETTI WITH FRESH ANCHOVIES

*Ingredients for 2 servings:*

**6 - 8 oz. thin spaghetti**
**4 salted anchovies**
**4 tablespoons extra-virgin olive oil**
**2 cloves garlic, peeled and crushed**

In a pot bring to a boil at least a quart of water with a pinch of salt. When the water boils add the pasta and stir.

While the pasta is cooking combine in a small pan the oil and garlic. Add the cleaned, boned anchovies.

(To clean the anchovies this is what I do: I take an anchovy and wipe the salt off with a paper towel. Then I take it and divide it in two along the backbone opening it like an apricot. Then I take the spine out from the tail to the head. It comes out easily. Try to take out all the bones. When cleaned in this way anchovies remain very tasty. I use them with a green sauce, with oil, in a dip, in tuna sauce, etc. If you rinse them instead, they lose much of their flavor. If you are lazy and want to buy anchovy fillets in jars in oil, fine, but they aren't as tasty and you run the risk of eating food with harmful preservatives. Even the oil used to preserve them certainly isn't extra-virgin olive oil: the only one guaranteed and healthy.)

Thus, clean the anchovies and put them in the pan together with the oil and garlic. Cook over very low heat, and slowly the anchovies will dissolve into a delicious grey sauce. It is easier to make than to write down! Be **careful not to make the sauce boil.** Now drain the spaghetti, season with the hot sauce, mix, and serve.

• This is a healthy, appetizing dish, excellent when you have little appetite, or an upset stomach, or nausea. It is not suitable to add Parmesan cheese.

★      ★      ★

## FUSILLI WITH OIL AND PARMESAN

*Ingredients for 2 servings:*

**6 oz. fusilli (pasta spirals)**
**4 tablespoons extra-pure olive oil**
**2 tablespoons Parmesan cheese**

In a pot with at least a quart of boiling, salted water cook the fusilli according to a package directions. Drain and season with raw oil and Parmesan cheese.

• This dish is light, good, and nutritious.

## POTATOES AND RICE

*Ingredients for 2 servings:*

**4 oz. rice**
**2 medium potatoes**
**2 tablespoons Parmesan cheese**

Peel the potatoes, cut them into cubes, and rinse them. Place the potatoes in a pan with a quart of cold water. Never cook starches in warm water. They'll remain grainy.

Add a teaspoon of salt, bring to a boil, and cook for 10 minutes—start timing when the water begins to boil.

After boiling for 10 minutes, add the rice, stir, and continue cooking over low heat for at least 15 minutes more. (It is better to let it cook uncovered.) After 15 minutes remove from heat, add the butter and Parmesan, and serve.

• This makes a good first course, easy and digestible. It is excellent even when reheated.

✶          ✶          ✶

## POTATO GNOCCHI WITH GORGONZOLA, FONTINA, OR MOZZARELLA CHEESE

*Ingredients for 2 servings:*

**8 oz. potato gnocchi**
**4 oz. gorgonzola, fontina, or mozzarella cheese**
**2 tablespoons butter**
**4 tablespoons Parmesan cheese**

Buy the gnocchi and the cheese of your choice. Bring to a boil 1 quart of salted water in a pot.

While the water is heating, cut the cheese into pieces and place them in a skillet together with 2 tablespoons of butter. Let the butter slowly melt. When the water boils add the gnocchi and stir well with a slotted spoon.

*Note:* As soon as the water again comes to a boil the gnocchi will rise to the surface. When this happens let the gnocchi boil for 1 minute only. With a slotted spoon take them out, putting them directly into the skillet with the butter and cheese. Add the Parmesan and serve.

• This is a delightful dish, cooked by mothers-in-law, but even you can easily create it if you buy the gnocchi already made.

★     ★     ★

## HEARTY STEAK

*Ingredients for 2 servings:*

**2 slices beef round steak 4 oz. each**
**4 slices prosciutto or bacon**
**4 leaves sage**
**2 tablespoons butter**

Prepare this hearty steak like this: sandwich the steak between the slices of prosciutto or bacon and the sage. Hold it all together with a wooden toothpick. Place the butter in a skillet and let it melt. To the melted butter add the steaks and brown them on one side. Then turn them with a flipper, add just a little salt (because the prosciutto or bacon is already salty). In all, let them cook for 5 minutes.

• This meat is nutritious and tasty, and it is even better, when accompanied by a tossed salad.

★     ★     ★

## TROUT WITH BUTTER AND SAGE

*Ingredients for 2 servings:*

**2 trout about ½ lb. each**
**1 tablespoon butter**
**2 tablespoons flour**
**1 sprig sage**

Buy 2 very fresh trout. They are fresh when the meat is firm and shiny: if they seem about to jump! Have them cleaned at the fish store, whose workers will usually do a better job than you can.

Wash the trout well, dry them with a clean paper towel, and coat them with flour. Do this by putting the flour in a dish, dredging the trout in the flour, and shaking off the excess.

Place the butter and sage in a skillet and let the butter melt. Add the trout, let it cook over high heat about 3 minutes. Turn the trout, add salt to taste, cover the pan, lower the heat to medium, and continue cooking another 5 minutes. Serve.

• This dish is excellent with any boiled vegetable or a salad. It can recharge the batteries of your memory thanks to the phosphorus it contains and is nutritious because of the protein it bestows on you.

★          ★          ★

## CALF LIVER IN BUTTER AND SAGE

*Ingredients for 2 servings:*

**4 slices calf liver**
**1 tablespoon butter**
**4 leaves sage**

Brown the butter and sage in a skillet, add the liver, and cook for 1 minute. Turn, add salt, and continue cooking the other side for 2 minutes. Now it's ready. You can eat it with a wonderful tossed salad.

When I say a tossed salad I mean, for example, tomatoes, peppers, fennel, celery, onion, etc.

• This is an excellent way of restoring very important vitamins and minerals, especially in the summer when you perspire more and you need energy without overloading your stomach.

## BAKED RABBIT FILLETS

*Ingredients for 2 servings:*

**4  slices rabbit fillet**
**1  pinch salt and pepper**
**1  sprig rosemary**

Buy 4 slices of rabbit fillet (the fillet is the center cut of a rabbit), but don't have the butcher pound them: that makes the meat tough! Take a casserole dish and line with aluminum foil.

Put the oven on high: 500°–550°F. While the oven is preheating lay the cutlets on the aluminum foil and sprinkle each with a little salt and pepper as well as the rosemary.

No other seasonings!

When the oven is hot, put the rabbit in the oven and leave it alone without turning for 15 minutes.

If you see that it is not well-browned, leave it 20 minutes total, but no more.

• You'll eat excellent, tasty meat that is easy to digest.

You can also cook in this way: turkey, chicken, beef or veal, brains, liver, lambs, swordfish steaks, fresh tuna, sardines, and whiting fillets. It is the healthiest way of cooking meat.

★    ★    ★

## TURKEY BUNDLES

*Ingredients for 2 servings:*

**4  slices turkey cutlets**
**1  small package dry porcini mushrooms**
**4  slices bacon or lard**
**2  tablespoons butter**

Place the mushrooms in warm water (it's convenient to put them in a little strainer); leave them there for 2–3 minutes. When they become soft, squeeze them (taking them in your hand and closing your fist).

Sandwich the turkey cutlet between slices of mushroom and roll it all up together with a strip of bacon. Prepare the rest of the turkey cutlets in the same manner.

Melt the butter in a pan and add the turkey bundles.

Cook for 3 minutes, turn, add salt to taste, and continue cooking another 3 minutes on the other side. Cover the pan and they are ready in 10 minutes, in all.

• This is a dish with an expert touch.

★    ★    ★

## HEALTHY STEAK

*Ingredients for 2 servings:*

**2  slices round steak**
**2  tablespoons olive oil**
**1  pinch salt**
**1  pinch pepper**

Heat a non-stick or iron skillet. When the skillet is hot add the meat without any seasonings. Cook over high heat for 1 minute. Using a wooden utensil, remove the meat from the pan to a dish. Heat the skillet again.

Again put the meat in the skillet and cook the other side for 1 minute. Remove the meat to a platter; over each slice put 1 tablespoon of oil to which the salt and pepper have already been added (put the oil, salt, and pepper in a cup and mix well with a fork).

● This is wholesome steak. The raw oil, salt, and pepper are very digestible.

★　　★　　★

## SKILLET FRESH FISH

*Ingredients for 2 servings:*

2 slices swordfish, fresh tuna, whiting, or sea bream, about 8 oz. each
1 pinch pepper
1 pinch salt

Heat a non-stick or iron skillet. When the pan is very hot add the fish of your choice. Let it cook for 3 minutes, turn, and continue cooking on the other side. Add salt and pepper.

● It is stupendous—without any other seasonings!

## STRING BEANS WITH CAPERS AND BASIL

*Ingredients for 2 servings:*

10 oz. string beans
1 tablespoon capers
4 leaves basil, chopped
4 tablespoons extra-virgin olive oil
   salt

Bring a quart of salted water to a boil. While waiting for the water to boil clean the beans, removing the 2 ends. Wash the beans.

*Note:* If you put the beans in cold water they'll cook just as well, but they'll turn yellow. Green vegetables are always cooked in boiling, salted water (string beans, zucchini, Swiss chard, Italian dandelion, etc.).

Let them cook for 20 minutes. Drain and put them in a bowl. Season with oil, capers in vinegar, and basil.

• They are delicious.

## STRING BEANS WITH MINT

Prepare the string beans as in the preceding recipe, substituting finely chopped mint for the capers and basil.

You can find mint at your green grocer.

## POTATOES WITH GREEN SAUCE

*Ingredients for 2 servings:*

10½ oz. potatoes
2 tablespoons parsley
1 tablespoon capers
2 anchovy fillets
4 tablespoons oil
1 tablespoon vinegar

Wash the potatoes leaving the skin on. Put the potatoes in a pot with 1 quart of cold water. Bring to a boil and boil for 20 minutes.

While the potatoes are cooking (it's better to leave the skin on because they retain more of their taste and don't fill up with water), wash the parsley: only the leaves, not the stems. Then chop the parsley together with the capers, anchovies, and a clove of garlic, if you like.

Having chopped all this together, put it in a bowl, add the oil and the vinegar, and mix.

Drain the potatoes, peel, and let them cool. Cut them into slices or cubes. Add the potatoes to the parsley mixture, add salt to taste, mix, and serve.

If it seems too complicated to mince the parsley, capers, anchovies, and garlic, put everything in the blender together with the oil and vinegar and blend. Then season the peeled, cut potatoes with the sauce prepared in the blender.

• It's all ready in 2 minutes.

★    ★    ★

## BASIL TOMATOES

*Ingredients for 2 servings:*

**10½ oz. salad tomatoes**
 **4 leaves basil**
 **2 tablespoons extra-virgin olive oil**

Wash the tomatoes and the basil, slice the tomatoes, and chop the basil. Put them in a glass bowl and season with a pinch of salt and the oil.

• This dish is rich in vitamins and minerals.

★    ★    ★

## RICH SALAD

*Ingredients for 2 servings:*

- 1 tomato
- 1 pepper
- 2 ribs celery
- 4 radishes
- 1 small onion
- 1 male fennel (the round ones, the long ones are female and more suited to boiling and grating)
- 4 oz. tuna
- 1 hard-boiled egg
- 1 tablespoon capers
- 4 tablespoons oil
- 1 tablespoon vinegar or lemon
- 2 pinches salt

Cook the egg (put the egg in cold water and let it boil for 7 minutes, calculating the cooking time from when the water begins to boil).

In the meantime, wash the vegetables, dry them, and cut them into small pieces.

Put all the vegetables in a bowl. Add the capers, the flaked tuna, and sliced egg. Add the salt, oil, and vinegar or lemon. Mix well.

● It's ready, and it can be a meal in itself, light and complete.

★　　★　　★

## CAPONATA

*Ingredients for 2 servings:*

**1 onion**
**1 tomato**
**1 eggplant**
**1 rib celery**
**2 peppers**
**2 potatoes**
**2 tablespoons oil**
**½ teaspoon salt**

This dish is a mother-in-law's little secret. It is a dish of long ago, and for this very reason it is appreciated. You can prepare it when your mother-in-law comes over, or when you just want to eat something different. However, it is also an intelligent way to use leftover or forgotten vegetables in the refrigerator. The vegetables can vary. The excellence of this dish is due to the variety in it.

Here's how to make it: wash all the vegetables. In a 2-quart saucepan heat the oil. To the oil add an onion, finely chopped. Sauté the onion over very low heat until golden in color. Now raise the heat and add the other vegetables, those that you have on hand or those that you like, cut into pieces. Mix well, cover, lower the heat, and continue cooking, stirring occasionally with a wooden spoon.

Let it cook like this for 45 minutes. Then add salt, stir again, remove from heat, and keep the pan covered for 5 minutes.

● This is an excellent dish. It goes well with grilled sausage, pork chops, but also other meats. It is not very suited to fish because the strong taste and smell threaten to overpower the delicacy of the fish.

★      ★      ★

## CELERY, POTATOES, AND TOMATOES

*Ingredients for 2 servings:*

8 oz. celery
8 oz. potatoes
8 oz. tomatoes
2 tablespoons butter
2 pinches salt

Peel the potatoes and wash them. Wash the celery and tomatoes.

Chop the celery; sauté the celery in the butter for 10 minutes. Cut the potatoes into cubes and add to the pan, mix, and continue cooking for another 10 minutes.

Add the sliced tomato, mix, add salt, and continue cooking for 15 minutes more. It's now ready.

• This is a delicate vegetable dish that goes well even with white meat: fish, rabbit, chicken, etc.

It's even better when reheated than when first made. When you make it, if you prepare a little extra it will be a job already done. You'll save yourself time, gas, and worry.

★        ★        ★

## ZUCCHINI, POTATOES, AND ONIONS

*Ingredients for 2 servings:*

8 oz. small zucchini
8 oz. or 2 medium potatoes
8 oz. or 2 medium onions
4 tablespoons oil
1 tablespoon lemon juice
1 teaspoon mustard (optional)

Peel the potatoes, wash them, and place them in a pot with 1 quart of salted, cold water. Bring to a boil.

When the potatoes boil, add the cleaned zucchini (when boiling zucchini you can just trim off the 2 ends). Peel the onions, trim off the ends, wash them, and add them to the potatoes and zucchini. Boil for 20 minutes.

Drain and cool the vegetables, then cut into cubes. Place them in a glass bowl with the seasoning prepared like this: the mustard, a pinch of salt, a tablespoon of vinegar or lemon, and oil. Stir with a fork. Add the boiled, cubed vegetables and toss. It's ready.

• This is a light, very good salad of boiled vegetables. You can even prepare it the day or night before. It is excellent with meat Alba style, cold roasts, trout in butter, or however you please. It's refreshing, diuretic, and purifies the system.

★     ★     ★

## TOMATOES AND MOZZARELLA

*Ingredients for 2 servings:*

2 tomatoes, about 6 oz. each
1 large mozzarella
1 pinch oregano
2 tablespoons extra-virgin olive oil
2 pinches salt

Wash the tomatoes and cut them into thin slices or cubes. Cut the mozzarella into thin slices or cubes.

Put the tomatoes and mozzarella in a glass bowl, season with oregano, salt, and oil, then mix and serve.

• This can be a complete meal.

★     ★     ★

## BRESAOLA, MOZZARELLA, AND GRAPEFRUIT

*Ingredients for 2 servings:*

6 oz. bresaola (a cured meat), sliced thin
1 mozzarella
1 lemon
2 tablespoons oil
1 pinch salt
1 pinch pepper
1 grapefruit

Place the slices of bresaola on a long oval platter. On each slice sprinkle a little salt, pepper, lemon, and oil. Cover with plastic wrap and refrigerate. It is better to prepare this the day before serving or 5-6 hours before, at least. Just before serving this dish add 2 strips of mozzarella, cut into wide but thin slices. Next to the mozzarella place slices of grapefruit prepared like this: peeled like an orange, cut into thin slices. On the grapefruit and mozzarella put a little pepper, salt, and oil.

• The result will be a tricolor dish with a new taste. It will be the high point of your solitary vacation and can welcome wives returning from the shore. They'll be happy to be home and will recount to everyone all your talents. Maybe next year they'll take you to the shore with them. . . ! This dish is good, youthful, invigorating, and satisfying.

★     ★     ★

## HARD-BOILED EGG SALAD

*Ingredients for 2 servings:*

8  oz. mixed salad greens (chicory, endive, young let-
    tuce, etc.)
3  eggs
1  tablespoon vinegar
4  tablespoons oil
1  small onion
2  pinches salt
1  pinch pepper

Put the eggs in a pot with cold water. Bring to a boil and let them boil for 7 minutes.

Remove from heat and put the pot under cold, running water. The eggs will cool quickly. Shell the eggs, slice or quarter them (there are egg slicers made just for this purpose). Clean and wash the chosen salad greens (those which you like best), drain, and place in a salad bowl.

Add the hard-boiled eggs, pepper, salt, vinegar, the sliced onion (if you don't like it you can omit it), and the oil. Mix it all together.

• It's a unique, nutritious, and easy dish.

✶　　　✶　　　✶

## OMELET WITH A TOSSED SALAD

*Ingredients for 2 servings:*

8  oz. tossed salad (celery, fennel, peppers, tomatoes;
    or a vegetable salad: whatever's in season)
3  eggs
3  tablespoons Parmesan cheese
3  sprigs parsley
3  sprigs basil
5  tablespoons oil
1  tablespoon vinegar or lemon juice
2  pinches salt

Put the eggs, salt, milk, and Parmesan in a vegetable dish. Vigorously beat the mixture with a fork for 5 minutes.

Add to this mixture the parsley and basil that have been rinsed and finely chopped. Now take a skillet, an iron skillet is most suited. Put 1 tablespoon of extra-virgin olive oil in the skillet and heat. When the oil is hot, pour in the mixture of eggs, Parmesan, milk, salt, basil, and parsley. Let this mixture cook for 3 minutes. Cover the skillet with a cover the same size.

Turn the omelet upside down onto the cover and place the omelet so turned in the skillet again, letting it cook for another 3 minutes on the other side. Remove from the heat: it's ready.

If you want a herbed omelet with a different taste, you can substitute mint (2 sprigs of 10 or 15 leaves), Swiss chard or chopped spinach instead of the parsley and basil. The basis remains the same, but the taste and aroma change.

● This is a tasty, light, and pleasing dish. The omelet is good even cold. You can accompany it with a tossed salad of your choice. A tossed salad is beneficial in offering you good taste and important substances. It is precious for its content of vitamins and minerals, which are important because they energize and stimulate the body. They're not fattening yet they renew the energy that cold and work consume.

## CHICKEN WITH OLIVES

*Ingredients for 2 servings:*

1 lb. of chicken cut into pieces (when using meat with bones it is good to calculate 8 oz. a person because you don't eat the bones)
4 oz. black or green olives
2 tablespoons oil
4 pinches salt
½ glass dry marsala

Put the chicken in a pan with the oil, and brown the chicken over high heat. When the chicken is well browned on all sides, add the salt and the dry marsala (I say dry marsala—not to be confused with the sweet one, which would be a horror!), as well as the olives. Cover, and let it cook over very low heat for 30 minutes.

*Note:* Instead of the chicken you can substitute rabbit, or even cod, or mackerel. It is equally good.

✷     ✷     ✷

## PEAS AND PROSCIUTTO

*Ingredients for 2 servings:*

7 oz. shelled peas (with the pods, 17½ oz.)
3½ oz. prosciutto
2 tablespoons butter
2 leaves sage
½ glass white wine

Shell the peas, put them in a small pan with the butter and sage, and sauté for 5 minutes. Add salt and dry white wine. Cover and continue cooking over very low heat for 10 minutes.

Add the prosciutto, which has been cut into strips (just roll the slices of prosciutto like a cigar and cut them like noodles), continue cooking, covered, over very low heat for another 10 minutes. They are ready.

● This can be a meal in itself, good, nutritious, and easy to digest.

★      ★      ★

## EGGS WITH BUTTER AND SMOKED BACON

*Ingredients for 2 servings:*

2 fresh eggs
1 tablespoon butter
4 slices smoked bacon
2 pinches salt

Melt the butter in a small pan over low heat and add the eggs being careful not to break the yolks.

Cover the pan and continue cooking for 2 or 3 minutes. Salt the eggs and then place 2 slices of bacon over each egg. Replace the lid and continue cooking for 1 minute longer. They are ready.

● They're appetizing, and you can accompany them with a cooked or raw tossed salad.

★      ★      ★

## BOILED ZUCCHINI WITH TUNA

*Ingredients for 2 servings:*

8 oz. fresh zucchini
6 oz. tuna in oil (don't buy canned tuna: it is inferior, has a lot of oil, you don't know if it's good, and you're paying for the packaging. It is always better to buy loose tuna, provided it is of good quality. Tuna is good when it is all in one piece, not oily, firm)
1 tablespoon oil
1 tablespoon salt
  a little lemon juice

Bring to a boil 2 cups salted water in a small pot. When the water boils add the zucchini, washed and ends removed.

Cook for 20 minutes. Drain and cool. When the zucchini have cooled slice them, add the flaked tuna, season with a little lemon juice and oil, and mix.

• This is a complete meal. The zucchini are poor nutritionally but refreshing, and the tuna is rich. Poor and rich together . . .

★　　　★　　　★

## ECONOMICAL PIZZA

*Ingredients for 2 servings:*

1 round loaf Tuscan bread (about 6 oz. or 4 slices stale bread)
4 peeled tomatoes or tomato sauce
1 mozzarella, 6 oz., or 4 slices fontina cheese
1 pinch oregano
4 anchovy fillets
2 tablespoon extra-virgin olive oil

It is appropriate to use stale bread, the Tuscan type because it is natural, but the recipe also works well with other stale bread.

Take the bread of your choice and on it put the peeled tomatoes crushed with a fork, or tomato sauce. Add the cheese cut into strips and the anchovies if you like them. Season with oregano and olive oil.

Cook the pizza in a 400° oven for 15 minutes.

• It's good and certainly cooked for the bread is already cooked. You can make it in very little time, and it's a good way of using stale bread.

★　　　★　　　★

## TOMINO CHEESE WITH GREEN SAUCE

*Ingredients for 2 servings:*

4 **fresh tomino cheeses**
4 **tablespoons extra-virgin olive oil**
1 **small bunch of parsley**
1 **tablespoon capers**
1 **tablespoon vinegar**
2 **pinches salt**
1 **pinch pepper**
   **anchovies, optional**

Place the cheeses in a dish and sprinkle each one with a little salt and pepper. On a cutting board place the trimmed and rinsed parsley and the capers. (If the capers are salted you must rinse them to remove the salt. It is always better to buy salted capers. They cost less, are more natural because they're preserved only with salt and not mysterious preservatives, and can be kept in a closed glass jar in the refrigerator.)

Chop the parsley and capers with a chopping knife. If you don't know how to use a chopping knife, you can use a steak knife to chop it all (as the butcher does when preparing raw chopped meat).

Put this chopped mixture into a bowl, add the oil and vinegar, mix well, and pour this sauce over each cheese. It is done! If you want you can add 2 cloves of garlic to the chopped mixture.

● This is an excellent, light dish and becomes a complete meal when accompanied by a tossed salad (it becomes even better if the salad has raw vegetables).

★     ★     ★

## TOMATOES STUFFED WITH TUNA SAUCE

*Ingredients for 2 servings:*

2 tomatoes, about 8 oz. each
4 oz. tuna
1 tablespoon capers
4 anchovy fillets
4 tablespoons extra-virgin olive oil
1 tablespoon lemon juice or vinegar

Wash and dry the tomatoes. Cut them in half. Empty out the tomatoes with the aid of a spoon.

In the blender put the scooped out tomato, the tuna, capers, anchovies, oil, and lemon juice or vinegar. Blend it all together to a smooth sauce. Refill the tomatoes with this sauce.

● It's easy, always turns out well, and is a dish that satisfies the growing need for a summer meal, wholesome and complete.

✱        ✱        ✱

## WHIMSICAL SALAD

*Ingredients for 2 servings:*

1 tomato
1 pepper
2 ribs celery
1 head fennel
2 oz. prosciutto
2 oz. frankfurters
2 oz. roast turkey
2 oz. cheese (berna or fontina, asiago, Swiss or mozzarella)
1 hard-boiled egg
2 oz. black olives
4 tablespoons oil
1 tablespoon lemon juice or vinegar
1 pinch pepper
2 pinches salt

Wash and dry the vegetables. Cut all the ingredients into cubes or thin slices and season with pepper, salt, oil, lemon or vinegar.

● This is a rich dish, complete in itself.

★        ★        ★

## OMELET WITH CHEESE AND SALAMI

*Ingredients for 2 servings:*

**3 fresh eggs**
**3 tablespoons grated Parmesan cheese**
**3 tablespoons milk**
**3 pinches salt**
**4 oz. sliced salami**
**2 tablespoons extra-virgin olive oil**

Put the eggs in a small bowl, add the Parmesan, milk, and salt. Beat with fork until well mixed.

Heat 1 tablespoon of oil in a non-stick or iron skillet. When the oil is hot, add the sliced salami (skinless), and heat the salami in a single layer, covering the bottom of the skillet. Now pour the beaten egg mixture on top of the salami.

Cover, and cook over medium heat until the mixture solidifies. With the help of the lid, turn the omelet. Put the remaining oil in the pan, return the turned omelet to the pan, and continue cooking 1 minute.

● It's delicious. Instead of salami you can substitute prosciutto, smoked bacon, mortadella, frankfurter, etc.)

★        ★        ★

## MEAT, ALBA STYLE

*Ingredients for 2 servings:*

2 **thinly sliced veal cutlets (about 3 oz. each)**
1 **porcini mushroom about 1 oz. or an equal amount**
   **of cultivated mushrooms**
1 **oz. Parmesan cheese**
1 **lemon**
   **oil**
   **salt**
   **pepper**

Place the 2 cutlets in a deep oval dish. Sprinkle with salt and pepper. Add the juice of 1 lemon and a little olive oil. Slice the mushrooms and the Parmesan and place them over the meat. Marinate for about 4-5 hrs.

● This is an excellent antipasto: a good, tasty, and nutritious cold dish. You need think no more about it because it's very digestible.

★    ★    ★

## SOLE IN WHITE WINE

*Ingredients for 2 servings:*

12 **oz. fillet of sole (make sure it's sole and not floun-**
    **der; they look alike but the flounder are less**
    **tasty, less nutritious, and less costly)**
1½ **tablespoon butter**
½ **glass dry white wine**
3 **pinches salt**
1 **pinch pepper**
1 **small bunch of sage, rosemary, and basil**
2 **leaves laurel**

Melt the butter in a small pot. Put 1 tablespoon of the melted butter in a roasting pan, add the slices of sole, sprinkle each with salt and pepper, and distribute the rest of the melted butter over the fillets. Add the white wine (spooning it over the slices).

Wash and dry the herbs and combine to make one bunch. Put it in the middle of the pan on top of the sole. Bake in a preheated oven at 400° for 20 minutes. It's now ready.

• This is a light dish, rich in phosphorus and important proteins. I suggest you accompany it with boiled potatoes seasoned with just a little salt and oil.

★    ★    ★

## MEAT PIZZAIOLA

*Ingredients for 2 servings:*

2 slices round steak, 3½ oz. each
4 peeled tomatoes
  basil
  parsley
  celery
  onion
  carrot
  rosemary
4 oz. fontina cheese
1 pinch oregano
2 capers
  a little dry white wine
  oil
  flour

Finely chop all of the herbs and sauté them in the oil in a skillet (the oil and herbs are put in the skillet together and then put on the heat). When the herbs are golden, coat the meat with flour and add it to the skillet with the herbs.

Let the meat and herbs brown together, add salt, then a little white wine. Let the wine evaporate, and add the peeled or fresh tomatoes, chopped. Cook for 2 or 3 minutes. Add the sliced fontina cheese, the capers, and the oregano.

Cover the pan and continue cooking for 5 minutes.

• This dish is very tasty and easy. However, you must follow the recipe carefully or it might be disappointing.

This procedure is good, also, for cooking chicken breasts or the whole chicken cut into pieces. In this case you must cook it at least 45 minutes. It's a very good way also to cook turkey breasts, hamburgers, quail, pheasant or guinea hen.

★     ★     ★

## VEAL WITH PROSCIUTTO

*Ingredients for 2 servings:*

2  **veal or beef cutlets about 4 oz. each**
4  **slices prosciutto or bacon**
   **sage**
1  **tablespoon butter**
   **toothpicks**

Cut each cutlet into 4 pieces. Also cut the prosciutto or bacon.

Take a small piece of meat and put a piece of prosciutto or bacon on top of and under it. Do the same with a leaf of sage. Hold it all together with a toothpick.

Melt the butter in a pan, add the meat, brown it first on one side and then the other. Add salt, just a little because the prosciutto or bacon is salty. Cook for no more than 5 minutes.

• If you substitute liver for the meat you will have an equally good and nutritious dish.

★     ★     ★

## ZUCCHINI WITH VINEGAR

*Ingredients for 2 servings:*

**1 lb. small fresh zucchini**
**1 onion**
**1 sprig rosemary**
**1 sprig sage**
**1 glass vinegar**
  **oil for frying, as much as needed**

Clean, wash, and dry the zucchini. If they're very small cut them only in half lengthwise. If they are a little bigger cut them into 4 pieces.

Put enough oil in a skillet (an iron one is best) and heat. When the oil is very hot (not burnt!), put in some of the zucchini. Let them become golden brown; they're cooked when they float on the oil. Remove them to a dish covered with a paper towel, and add salt. Cook the rest of the zucchini in the same way. When all the zucchini have been fried, pour the oil into a container (it can be used again to fry potatoes or other vegetables).

Wipe the skillet with a paper towel to clean it well, and put in a little olive oil. Heat the oil, then add the onion finely chopped, the sprigs of sage and rosemary, and, if you like, 2 cloves of garlic. Sauté to a golden color, add the vinegar, and let it boil 2 minutes.

Put the fried zucchini in a container with a lid, and pour the vinegar and warmed herbs over them. Let them cool, and enjoy this stimulating vegetable.

• You can prepare many zucchini like this, because they can be kept even 20 days covered in the refrigerator. They serve as a side dish to roasts and can even be eaten in rolls.

You can make fish in this way (tench, sardines, eel) and also sliced pumpkin.

★      ★      ★

# 2

## WHEN THE FAMILY HAS THE FLU

Sometimes the flu occurs as a veritable infectious epidemic. Many times you hear: "We're all in bed with the flu."

If you are this unfortunate and poorly organized (since good organization foresees even a change in duties), the flu does what it wills. If no one is well who can go out and has the will of strength to cook, certainly it will be hard. It may be necessary to make peace with your mother-in-law. . . .

If none of this is possible, the only thing left is to get better, and fast.

To get well one needs a healthy diet. I have written some menus for 7 days. I hope it's enough; if not, start again from the beginning.

It is important to know some good caterers, able to serve you at home, in case of necessity. It is important to have friends, among the neighbors, as well as the caterers. If not, you might have to call 911 and risk having them charge you with abandoning and not feeding your family!

I have selected nutritious, light, and energizing dishes. Help yourselves if you want others to help you.

★    ★    ★

### POTATOES AND RICE

Ingredients for 1 serving:

1  small potato
2  tablespoons rice
1  tablespoon Parmesan cheese
   a little butter
   salt, as much as needed

Peel the potatoes, wash and dice.

45

Put the potatoes in a pot and add 2 cups of cold water for each person (medium tea cups). Add salt and cook for 10 minutes (begin timing when the water boils).

Add the rice, stir, and continue cooking another 15 minutes (again begin timing when the mixture recommences boiling). Remove from heat and add a little butter and Parmesan. Mix and serve.

● This is a first course that is very nutritious and healthy. The butter and Parmesan added at the end, raw, remain more digestible. If you want to make this a complete meal (when you're flu-ridden you have little appetite, but it is important to nourish yourself in order to be stronger than the flu virus!), add, always at the end of cooking, 2 egg yolks, or some mozzarella or fontina cheese, diced. With the heat they'll melt, disappear from sight, but not from the stomach which will sort it all out bestowing on you strength and health.

★　　★　　★

## RICE, TOMATOES, AND BASIL

*Ingredients for 1 serving:*

**3 oz. rice, approximately**
**1 ripe tomato**
**1 sprig basil**
**1 tablespoon oil**
**1 tablespoon Parmesan cheese (optional)**
**1 teaspoon salt**

Bring to a boil a pot of salted water. When the water boils add the rice, stir, bring to a boil again, and cook over high heat uncovered for 15 minutes.

In the meantime, wash the tomato and basil and chop them. Drain the rice and return to the pot; season with the chopped tomato and basil and oil.

Let it all heat through. It's ready! If you like you can add Parmesan cheese.

• The oil and tomatoes that have just been warmed (they should not boil) are digestible and retain precious vitamins besides important minerals needed to fight the flu (tomatoes contain much vitamin C, which is anti-flu). The vegetable richest in vitamin C is raw pepper: if you like you can substitute peppers for the tomatoes, provided they are home-grown and ripen on the plant, and the doctor will come to recuperate at your house.

★    ★    ★

## JULIAN CREAM SOAP

*See Index.*

★    ★    ★

## ENERGIZING SOUP

*See Index.*

★    ★    ★

## RICE AND PEAS

*Ingredients for 1 serving:*

**2 oz. shelled peas**
**2 oz. rice**
**1 tablespoon Parmesan cheese**
**½ glass white wine**
**a little butter**
**enough water to cook everything**

Clean the peas. Put them in a pot large enough to hold peas and rice for the whole family.

Add a little butter to the peas, sauté the peas in the butter for 11 minutes, add the rice and the white wine, and stir until the wine evaporates. Salt the rice and peas with a pinch of salt per person.

Cover the rice and peas with boiling water (it is good to start a pot of water boiling when you start cooking the peas). Stir occasionally, and when the water is absorbed add more. Continue cooking for about 15 minutes. Remove from heat, and add a little more butter and the Parmesan cheese.

● Here you have a dish that can be a sufficient meal for patients. To complete the nutritional value of this meal, plenty of good fruit is all you need.

★          ★          ★

## CREAMED ZUCCHINI WITH BASIL

*Ingredients for 1 serving:*

4  oz. fresh zucchini
2  oz. milk or water
6  leaves basil
1  tablespoon Parmesan cheese
1  pinch salt
   a little butter

After cutting the ends off the zucchini wash them.

In a pot put the milk or (if you don't like or can't digest milk) water. When it boils add the salt, then add the sliced zucchini. Continue cooking for 15 minutes.

Remove from heat, and add the washed basil leaves, the butter, and the Parmesan. If you have a blender, blend it all together. A new, light, refreshing zucchini cream is ready. If you don't have a blender or food processor, whip with an electric mixer.

● It's ready, light, easy to digest and chew. It's low in calories, so it's better to complete the meal with grilled meat or fish or cheese and vegetables or fruit.

★          ★          ★

## BREAD AND BASIL SOUP

*Ingredients for 1 serving:*

1 **tablespoon crushed bread**
1 **tablespoon Parmesan cheese**
1 **cup water**
2 **leaves basil**
  **a little butter or oil**
  **a little salt**

Heat the salted water in a pot. When the water boils add the bread, stir, and cook for 5 minutes (the bread is already cooked).

Remove from heat, add the washed, chopped basil, the Parmesan, and the butter or oil. It's ready.

● This is a wholesome, nutritious soup.

## RICE AND MILK

*Ingredients for 1 serving:*

1 **glass rice**
2 **glasses milk**
1 **pinch salt**
  **a little butter**
  **Parmesan cheese to taste**

Heat the milk to boiling in a pot, add salt, add the rice, stir occasionally, and continue cooking, uncovered, over low heat for 20 minutes.

Remove from heat and season with butter and Parmesan.

● This is a nutritious dish. It is best not to accompany it with meat or fish. The fruit shouldn't be acidic, therefore, no oranges, tangerines, or grapefruit. An apple or a sweet seasonal fruit is better.

✱       ✱       ✱

## SEMOLINA WITH MILK

*Ingredients for 1 serving:*

**1 cup milk**
**1 tablespoon semolina**
**butter**
**a little Parmesan to taste**
***Variant:* instead of the cheese use a tablespoon of**
**sugar and a little salt**

Bring the milk to a boil in a pot (keep the pot uncovered and watch the pot otherwise it will overflow) and add salt.

Add the semolina little by little. Stir continuously for 20 minutes. Cook over very low heat and if it sticks don't worry; it's not possible to prevent. Remove from heat and season with butter and Parmesan or sugar.

• This is a very nutritious soup. It's easy to digest. If you want to make it even more nutritious, you can add 2 or 3 egg yolks when you remove it from the heat, stirring vigorously. The eggs are neither seen nor tasted, but their nutritious value is guaranteed. The less eggs are cooked the more digestible they are. The semolina is calming and facilitates sleep. Also, after a dish of semolina made like this some fresh fruit is all that's needed. If you don't care for fruit, some fresh cheese or prosciutto is good.

## SPAGHETTI, TOMATOES, AND BASIL

*Ingredients for 1 serving:*

**3 oz. spaghetti**
**1 plum tomato**
**4 leaves basil**
**1 tablespoon olive oil**
**1 pinch salt**

Bring to a boil a pot of salted water. When the water boils add the spaghetti, stir well to separate the spaghetti, and cook for as long as package instructions direct.

In the meantime, wash the tomato and the basil and chop them. Drain the spaghetti and season it with tomato, basil, oil, and Parmesan.

• This dish is appetizing, light, and full of vitamins!

After the spaghetti don't eat red meat (veal, beef, lamb) but white meat, which is more digestible and doesn't clash with the first course.

★    ★    ★

## SOLE WITH BUTTER

*Ingredients for 1 serving:*

**1 sole**
**1 leaf sage**
**a little butter**

Melt the butter in a pan, add the sage, and sauté. Add the sole that has been cleaned and washed or if you prefer, you can buy fillet of sole already cleaned (but it may not be as good or as nutritious). Let the sole brown for 2 minutes on one side, turn with care so as not to break it, add salt, and brown another 2 minutes on the other side. It's ready.

• This is excellent when accompanied by a carrot salad, seasoned with oil and lemon or with boiled zucchini, boiled beans, etc.

★    ★    ★

## VEAL, ALBA STYLE

*Ingredients for 1 serving:*

1 **veal cutlet, at least 3 oz.**
1 **tablespoon oil**
1 **pinch pepper**
1 **pinch salt**
1 **or 2 fragments of Parmesan or an equal amount of porcini mushrooms or cultivated mushrooms**
1 **tablespoon lemon juice**

Put the slices of veal in a pan and season with pepper, salt, lemon, oil; then put a second layer of veal on top and season.

Keep layering the veal and seasoning it until it is all used up. Leave the meat for several hours. I prepare it the night before for the next day. When you are ready to serve it, take the slices of meat, arrange them on a serving platter in a single layer, and with a chopping knife chop the cheese or mushrooms and sprinkle over the meat. Season it all with the remaining juice in the pan. It's ready.

● This is a wholesome, nutritious, and appetizing dish. If you have difficulty chewing, use chopped veal instead of veal slices and proceed in the same manner.

In that case, though, you make one layer of chopped meat and season as with the whole slices. When ready to serve add the mushrooms or Parmesan thinly sliced.

## GRILLED OR BAKED RABBIT FILLET

*Ingredients for 1 serving:*

1 **piece rabbit fillet, at least 6 oz.**
1 **sprig rosemary**
1 **pinch salt and pepper on each piece**

If cooking the fillet on the barbecue or grill, light the grill, lay the meat on the hot grill, add only rosemary, and brown the meat on both sides. Remove it from the heat to a platter and season with salt and pepper: no other condiments!

When baking in the oven proceed like so: lay the meat in a baking dish lined with aluminum foil. On each piece of meat sprinkle a little pepper, salt, and a sprig of rosemary. Bake in a very hot oven (475°) for 15 minutes.

- This method of cooking meat has good results. You have a wholesome and nutritious dish, easy to digest.

★     ★     ★

## LIVER WITH BUTTER AND SAGE

*Ingredients for 1 serving:*

1 slice calf liver, 3-4 oz.
1 sprig sage
1 pinch salt
  a little butter

Put a little butter and the sage together in a skillet, add the liver, and cook over medium heat.

It's enough to cook the liver for 1 minute on each side. When the liver is brown, add salt. It's ready.

- Liver is very nutritious and invigorating. The less it cooks the more tender and digestible it is.

★     ★     ★

## TURKEY MORSELS

*Ingredients for 1 serving:*

1 piece of turkey, at least 2 oz.
1 slice prosciutto
1 sprig sage
1 pinch salt
  a little butter

Take a small, thick piece of turkey (dark or white meat) and wrap it with a slice of prosciutto or bacon.

Put the butter and sage in a skillet, add the prepared turkey morsels, and brown them; add salt and cover the skillet. They are ready in 10 minutes.

• Turkey is white meat but it's dry. That's why I advise you to wrap it with prosciutto or bacon. It is easy to digest, relatively nutritious, and good.

★      ★      ★

## VEAL SCALLOPINI WITH LEMON

*Ingredients for 1 serving:*

1 veal cutlet about 4 oz.
1 pinch salt
1 tablespoon lemon juice
  some grated lemon peel
  a little oil
  a little flour

Take the slices of meat, cut off the little skin around them with a sharp knife (otherwise when cooking, the skin will shrink pulling the meat closed like a bowl), and coat each slice with flour.

Having prepared the slices in this manner, take a skillet, put in a little oil, heat, and fry the floured slices of veal in the hot oil.

Brown and salt each slice, sprinkle on a little lemon juice and grated lemon peel—just a few flakes on each slice.

*Note:* When grating the lemon skin it is important to wash the lemon well, It's wise to wash the lemon in water and bicarbonate, rinse, dry, and then use the lemon. Cover the pan and continue cooking over very low heat for 10 minutes.

• You'll have tender, tasty meat, easy to digest.

★      ★      ★

## VEAL SCALLOPINI WITH OLIVES

*Ingredients for 1 serving:*

1 veal cutlet, 3 oz.
1 tablespoon black olives
½ glass dry marsala
1 pinch salt
  a little oil
  flour, as much needed

Cut the external skin from the meat, and flour each slice.

Heat a skillet with a little oil, brown the meat on both sides, and add salt. Add the olives and the marsala, cover the pan, and cook over very low heat for 10 minutes. It's ready.

● This is an appetizing and tender dish.

## BAKED CALF BRAINS

*Ingredients for 1 serving:*

4 oz. calf brains
1 sprig rosemary for each slice
1 pinch salt and pepper for each slice
1 sheet aluminum foil

Remove the outer membrane of the brains (it's simple: soak the brains in tepid water and pull it off with your hands), wash the brains under cold, running water and dry them.

Put the brains on a cutting board and with a sharp knife, cut slices about 1 inch thick. Take a baking dish and line it with aluminum foil. Lay the slices of calf brains on the foil, season with salt, pepper, and rosemary. No other condiments are needed. Bake in a hot preheated oven at 475° for 15 minutes. It's ready.

• Brains are rich in phosphorus, nutritious, and easy to digest. You can add a little lemon juice when they're almost done. It's good for you!

★        ★        ★

## VEAL STEAK

*Ingredients for 1 serving:*

**1 veal steak
1 tablespoon oil
1 pinch salt and pepper**

Heat a griddle or iron skillet and then add the meat. Cook 1 minute on each side. Remove to a serving platter.

In a separate bowl combine the salt, pepper, and oil, and mix well. Pour over the steak. It's ready.

• You'll have meat that is nutritious and easy to digest; the raw oil is good for you, the pepper is anti-flu! If you prefer, you can just add salt and oil.

## BOILED POTATOES AND STRING BEANS

*Ingredients for 1 serving:*

**2 oz. potatoes**
**2 oz. string beans**
**1 tablespoon olive oil**
**1 pinch salt**
  **vinegar or lemon juice to taste**

Peel the potatoes, wash them, put them in a pot covered with cold water, and add salt. Bring to a boil.

In the meantime, trim the top and tails off the beans, wash them, and add them to the boiling potatoes. Boil the vegetables for 20 minutes, starting from when the water begins to boil. When the potatoes cool, cut them in pieces, add the string beans, and season with a little salt and oil and some vinegar or lemon juice if you like. Toss. It's ready.

• This is a light and nutritious salad.

If you cook the beans in cold water they will become yellow, ugly, and not very appetizing; all green vegetables should be cooked in boiling, salted water.

## BOILED ONIONS OR CARROTS

*Ingredients for 1 serving:*

**4 oz. onions or carrots**
**1 teaspoon chopped parsley**
**1 pinch capers**
**1 salted anchovy**
**1 tablespoon oil and vinegar**
  **little salt because the sauce is already salty**

Clean the onions or carrots and place them in a pot of boiling, salted water.

Boil the vegetables (15 minutes for the onions, 20 minutes for the carrots). While the vegetables are cooking, wash the parsley (only the leaves), dry, put it on the cutting board with the salted anchovy (naturally wiped of its salt and deboned) and the capers. Chop these ingredients very fine with a chopping knife.

Remove to a bowl, season with oil and vinegar, and mix. If you want to get done faster put the parsley, capers, anchovy, oil, and vinegar in the blender. Blend it all together. Now, drain the vegetables, cool, cut into pieces, season with a little olive oil, and mix. Lastly, add the prepared sauce and mix well. It's ready.

• This is a stimulating and pleasing salad. The vitamin C in the fresh parsley makes it a therapeutic dish; vitamin C is anti-flu. It's good for you, and you'll eat it with gusto.

★    ★    ★

## POTATOES WITH MILK AND CHEESE

*Ingredients for 1 serving:*

3½ oz. potatoes
1 tablespoon Parmesan cheese
1 slice mozzarella or fontina cheese (1 oz.)
½ glass milk
1 tablespoon butter
1 pinch salt

Peel the potatoes, wash and dry them, and cut them in thin slices.

Lightly grease a pan with butter, put a layer of sliced potatoes in the pan, sprinkle with a little salt and Parmesan, and dot with butter. Spread slices of cheese on top and add a little milk.

Make a second or third layer like the first. End with a layer of Parmesan, butter, cheese, and milk. Bake in a hot oven at 475° for at least 45 minutes.

• This dish can be a complete supper meal or a side dish for grilled meat, liver, brains, etc.

★          ★          ★

## ROMAN STYLE PEAS

*Ingredients for 1 serving:*

**3½ oz. fresh or frozen peas
1 oz. prosciutto
1 sprig sage
½ glass white wine
1 pinch salt
 a little butter**

Put the butter and sage in a pot, melt the butter, sauté the peas, add salt and dry white wine.

Let the wine evaporate, cover the pot, and cook for 20 minutes. Take the slices of prosciutto, roll them together forming a single roll of prosciutto, and cut it into strips. Add the prosciutto to the peas. Continue cooking 5 minutes more. It's ready.

• This dish can be a complete supper meal. All that's needed to complete the necessary nutrients is some fresh fruit in season.

## BOILED TROUT WITH LEMON

*Ingredients for 1 serving:*

1 **trout about 6 oz.**
1 **sprig rosemary**
1 **sprig sage**
1 **rib celery**
1 **small bunch basil and parsley**
1 **onion**
1 **glass white wine**
1 **tablespoon lemon juice**
1 **tablespoon olive oil**
  **salt**
  **pepper (optional)**

In a fish kettle or a saucepan combine a glass of water and a glass of wine.

Add the washed, aromatic herbs leaving them whole, then add a little salt. Bring to a boil and add the cleaned trout. Boil for 5 minutes (starting from when the water begins boiling again). Remove the fish. It's ready to serve. Cut open each trout, take out the backbone, and season with a little salt, pepper, oil, and lemon juice.

• Whiting, salmon, John Dory, and sole can also be cooked in this way. It's an intelligent way of making fish. The aromatic herbs and the white wine make the fish more tasty. It is a healthy, nutritious, and light dish. You can even use mayonnaise or aurora sauce as dressing.

## TUNA SAUSAGE

*Ingredients for 1 serving:*

3½ **oz. tuna in oil**
  1 **tablespoon Parmesan cheese**
  1 **tablespoon crushed bread**
  1 **egg**

Drain the tuna well, put the tuna through a meat grinder, and put it in a bowl. Add the egg, bread, and Parmesan, then mix well. With the resulting paste form a roll. Take a clean cloth or linen napkin, roll this large "sausage," and tie it up as if it were a roast beef. Bring a little pot of water to a boil and add a little salt.

When the water boils add the "sausage" and cook over minimum heat for 20 minutes. Remove from the pot. It's ready.

• This is very good and nutritious. You can eat it as it is or seasoned with oil and lemon, or mayonnaise.

## TOMINO CHEESE WITH OIL AND LEMON

*Ingredients for 1 serving:*

1 or 2 tomino cheeses
1 pinch salt and pepper for each cheese
1 tablespoon lemon juice
1 tablespoon olive oil

Put the tomino cheese in a plate, and season with salt, pepper, lemon, and oil. They're ready.

• Tasty, light, wholesome.

## PROSCIUTTO ROLLS

*Ingredients for 1 serving:*

2 slices prosciutto
1 oz. berna cheese
1 oz. carrots
1 pinch salt
1 tablespoon oil
  lemon juice, as much as needed

Peel the carrots, wash and slice them as for salad, or grate them.

Season the carrots with salt, lemon, and oil. Chop or grate the berna, too.

Lay a slice of prosciutto on the cutting board, then take a spoonful of carrots and place them in the middle of the slice of prosciutto; now take a spoonful of berna and place it next to the carrots. Roll up the prosciutto forming little bundles. It's done.

● This is a nutritious dish, easy to make; it can be considered a complete meal.

★　　★　　★

## POACHED EGG

*Ingredients for 1 serving:*

**1 egg**
**½ pan water**
**1 tablespoon vinegar**
**1 pinch salt**

Fill a small pot half full of hot water. Add the salt and vinegar.

Bring to a boil. When the water boils, lower the heat. Take the egg, crack it open, and put it in the boiling water. Raise the heat and boil until the egg white coagulates (about 5 minutes).

Remove the egg with a slotted spoon. It's ready.

● Cooked in this way the egg becomes easy to digest and is tasty. The yolk remains almost raw, therefore, more digestible. It can be eaten just so, or dressed with a little tomato sauce and anchovies.

★　　★　　★

## BOILED RABBIT

*Ingredients for 1 serving:*

1 **piece of rabbit about 6 oz.**
1 **rib celery**
1 **onion**
1 **sprig rosemary**
1 **leaf laurel**
   *To season:* **oil, lemon, salt, pepper, small raw onions, various sauces.**

Heat to boiling a pot with 1 quart of water, then add the washed vegetables and 1 tablespoon of salt. When the water boils add the washed rabbit. Simmer over low heat for at least 1 hour. Remove the meat and season the piece of rabbit with a little salt, pepper, oil, lemon, and some slices of raw onion.

• It's excellent, tasty, easy to digest. If you like you can eat it just boiled without dressing or accompanied by various sauces like: catsup, mayonnaise, mustard, horseradish, and green sauce. The strained broth is excellent for soup or risotto.

★    ★    ★

## BAKED APPLES

*Ingredients for 1 serving:*

2 **apples**
1 **tablespoon sugar for each apple**

Wash and dry the apples. With an apple corer, remove the core leaving the rest of the apple whole.

Put the apples in a baking pan or casserole dish (if using a casserole dish, line with aluminum foil) and put the sugar in the center of each apple. Bake in a hot oven at 475° for at least 1 hour. They're ready and good.

● I don't put water or anything else on the apples, only the sugar. Cooked like this they remain a little dry and are just sweet enough.

## COOKED PEARS

*Ingredients for 1 serving:*

**2 pears**
**2 tablespoons sugar for each pear**
**1 glass water**
**1 glass white wine**
**2 whole cloves**
**1 cinnamon stick**

Wash the pears well and dry them.

Put 2 tablespoons of sugar in a pot. (Simply leave the pot with the sugar over minimum heat until the sugar melts and turns a golden color.)

Add the pears (whole and with the skin), then the wine and water. Sprinkle the rest of the sugar over the pears and add the cloves and cinnamon stick. Cover the pot and continue cooking for 1 hour.

● They are very good.

## ORANGES, TANGERINES, OR BANANAS WITH SUGAR AND LEMON

*Ingredients for 1 serving*

**1 orange**
**1 tablespoon sugar**
**1 tablespoon lemon juice**

Peel the orange, also removing the white part. Cut into thin slices.

Put the slices in a deep rectangular pan and sprinkle each layer of oranges with sugar and lemon juice.

● This is a vitamin-packed, energizing dish.

As with all fruit it is best to eat this dish at mid-morning or in the afternoon, between meals.

# 3

# WHEN YOUR TEETH RETIRE

*It can happen that someone in your family needs to wear dentures. This is an unpleasant fact. Some people calmly accept them as they accept their pension. Teeth may "retire," but given the fact that they are necessary to live well, to digest, and to smile with an open heart, this experience is an important time for the family. Thus, something must be done so that the person waiting for new teeth feels that the whole family is behind him or her.*

*It should be something done spontaneously that lets the family recover one of its blessings.*

*I suggest a menu that can be eaten by the entire family.*

*It is best not to make more trouble with separate "little pots." Your relative needs food easy to eat. For you there's the advantage of not having to chew so much. You'll do less work and feel united even in pap.*

★　　　★　　　★

**PASTA AND CHEESE SOUP**

*Ingredients for 1 serving:*

1　tablespoon grated Parmesan cheese
1　tablespoon fresh bread crumbs
1　grated lemon rind
1　pinch salt
1　teaspoon oil
1　pinch nutmeg
1　egg
1　cup beef stock
　 grated bread

Combine the bread crumbs and Parmesan in a bowl, then add the egg, salt, lemon rind, nutmeg, and oil.

66

Mix well with a wooden spoon. The resulting mixture should be soft but consistent, a little firmer than mashed potatoes. Let the mixture rest for 3 or 4 hours.

Heat the beef broth (a good broth: to put this pasta in bouillon is a real profanation). When the broth boils, add the pasta, called "passatelli," a little at a time.

To make the "passatelli" you need a special press that you can buy in houseware stores. It may be necessary to order it as it is a special item. Not having the right tool is no reason not to make "passatelli." You can use a potato ricer instead.

Put a ball of dough the size of a medium potato in the ricer and squeeze the "passatelli" directly into the boiling broth. Then continue with the dough in this manner cooking them in the broth until no more dough is left. When the last of the "passatelli" have been put in the broth, turn off the heat. They're ready.

● This is a nutritious soup, easy to digest. It can be considered a complete meal provided you eat some fresh seasonal fruit at the same meal.

★     ★     ★

## ANGEL HAIR PASTA WITH OIL AND BASIL

*Ingredients for 2 servings:*

**6 oz. angel hair pasta (capelli d'angelo)**
**2 tablespoons oil**
**2 tablespoons Parmesan cheese**
**1 pinch basil**

Bring to a boil 2 quarts of water and add 1 tablespoon of salt.

When the water boils add the pasta, stir, and cook 2 minutes. Drain and season with chopped basil, raw oil, and Parmesan.

★     ★     ★

## CREAM OF CHICKEN SOUP

*Ingredients for 2 servings:*

**6 oz. fresh cream**
**4 oz. boiled skinless chicken**
**2 tablespoons butter**
**1 tablespoon flour**
**1 egg**
**½ qt. beef broth**
   **salt**

Melt the butter in a small heavy saucepan, add the flour stirring with a wooden spoon, then slowly add the broth stirring constantly.

Having added all the broth, lower the heat to minimum and cook for 20 minutes. In the meantime grind or blend (in a blender) the chicken. When the broth has simmered for 20 minutes, add the blended chicken, stir, and add half the cream. Then turn off the heat.

In a soup tureen combine an egg yolk and the remaining cream and beat with a fork. Slowly add the hot soup, mix, and serve.

● It is stupendous, nutritious, and sufficient to nourish you in a wholesome way. Don't forget the vitamins you get from some precious seasonal fruit.

## POLENTA AND CHEESE SAUCE

*Ingredients for 2 servings:*

**6 oz. corn meal**
**1 qt. water**
**1 tablespoon oil**
   **salt**

Bring to a boil a pot with 1 quart of salted water.

When the water boils add the oil and corn meal (the corn meal is added bit by bit), slowly stirring with a whisk or wooden spoon. When all the flour has been added continue cooking for at least 20 minutes, stirring occasionally.

Now put the polenta into a mold with a hole in the center (one used for puddings or flan). Let the polenta cool a little so that it sets well. Put the mold with the polenta in the oven.

★       ★       ★

## CHEESE SAUCE

*Ingredients for 4 servings:*

**14 oz. fontina cheese**
**4 egg yolks**
**enough milk to cover the cheese**

Cut the fontina into thin slices and put it in a heavy saucepan.

Cover the fontina with boiling water (I use it to make the polenta: I let the water boil with the fontina for 1 minute, then I pour the boiling water in the pot where I'm making the polenta; this way I don't waste anything).

Drain off the boiling water and cover the softened fontina with milk, just enough to cover the fontina. Put the pot over minimum heat and stir continuously with a wooden spoon until the fontina and milk are amalgamated.

Now, remove from heat and add the egg yolks, one at a time, stirring vigorously. When all 4 yolks have been added return the pot to the heat and let the cheese sauce coagulate. It's simple but must be done correctly; the sauce must never boil, only thicken. Now remove the polenta from the oven and unmold it onto a round platter. Pour the cheese sauce in the hole in the middle of the mold and serve warm.

● This is an elegant, nutritious dish, a meal in itself. All you need to complete the menu is a good serving of fresh fruit.

★      ★      ★

## CREAM OF SPINACH SOUP

*Ingredients for 2 servings:*

**9 oz. fresh spinach**
**9 oz. milk**
**4 oz. cream**
**2 heaping tablespoons Parmesan cheese**
**1 tablespoon flour**
   **salt**

Trim and wash the spinach and cook it in a pot without any water, just a pinch of salt, for 10 minutes.

The cooking spinach will release some water; drain the spinach saving this water. Cool the spinach under running water, squeeze it, and put it through a vegetable grinder or in a blender. Melt the butter in a heavy saucepan. Add the flour to the melted butter; stir well to a smooth consistency without lumps. Add cold or warm milk a little at a time making a white sauce.

Stir continuously until the mixture becomes homogeneous. Add the ground spinach, stir, add the water retained from the cooked spinach, and add the cream. Continue cooking for 10 minutes. Remove from heat, add the Parmesan cheese, mix, and serve.

● This is a nutritious soup, easy to digest thanks to the milk that neutralizes the acids.

★      ★      ★

## CREAM OF TOMATO SOUP

*Ingredients for 2 servings:*

**9 oz. ripe meaty tomatoes**
**3½ oz. cream**
**9 oz. milk**
**2 tablespoons butter**
**1 tablespoon flour**
**1 sprig basil**
**1 pinch sugar and salt**

Clean and wash the tomatoes, chop them, and remove the seeds. Put the tomatoes in a small pot with 1 tablespoon of butter and the washed basil.

Cook over low heat, stirring frequently. In the meantime, melt 1 tablespoon of butter in a heavy pot. When the butter has melted add 1 tablespoon of flour; stir to blend the butter and flour without lumps. Then add the milk a little at a time stirring continuously.

When the milk has been added, continue cooking for 10 minutes, then add to this white sauce the tomatoes (which have been put through a vegetable grinder or blender). Add a pinch of sugar (the sugar neutralizes the acid in the tomatoes); stir and add the cream (fresh cream is best rather than packaged cream, which only heaven knows how it's made). It's ready.

• This is a stupendous soup, pleasing and nutritious. It can be served with bread toasted in the oven—not fried in butter or oil, but only in the oven.

★    ★    ★

## CREAM OF ASPARAGUS SOUP

*Ingredients for 2 servings:*

17½  oz. asparagus
10½  oz. beef stock
 3½  oz. cream
  1  tablespoon butter
  1  tablespoon flour
  2  tablespoons Parmesan cheese
    salt

Scrape the asparagus stalks with a knife, wash them well, and snap off and discard the white part of the stalk, which is tough and of no use.

Put the beef stock in a pot with an equal amount of water and add salt. When the water boils add the asparagus.

Drain the asparagus, reserving the broth. In the meantime, prepare a white sauce with 1 tablespoon of butter and 1 tablespoon of flour, then dilute it with the cooking water reserved from the asparagus.

Cook over low heat stirring occasionally. Add the tender asparagus tips to the white sauce. In a blender, blend the rest of the asparagus stalks and add this to the white sauce, add the cream, and boil for 1 minute. Remove from heat and add the Parmesan.

● It's ready, excellent, light, but contraindicated for people with kidney problems.

# 4

## WHEN THE HOUSEKEEPER QUITS

*This is an occasion to calmly think about the things that you used to see your mother do at home.*

*Stir up your memory, your spirit of observation, and you'll see how many things come to mind.*

*It's better to recall the time you lived with your family, not the times when you returned for a visit, or still return today as a pastor, because now, when you go home your mother certainly prepares special dishes.*

*Surely you merit special dishes because you are somewhat of a "super mover," a person with many responsibilities. He who dedicates himself to others cannot have personal problems; I'm not saying that you shouldn't be hungry, but you should not mourn over the things you long for. You must always be in good form, serene, and available.*

*A good and healthy diet helps all this. If then you have no needs, if all goes well because you are calm and optimistic, because other values make you calm, so much the better. It will all be easier. Finally, if you want to feed yourself dishes that you remember this is a good occasion to do so.*

*It will give you a better understanding of families and single people, and you will be a teacher even in these cases. Experience the joy of remaining calm with a secret talent that you feared you didn't have.*

*Now that the housekeeper has quit you may feel lost and unable to do anything. You may have the confused idea that occupying yourself with cooking is time lost, a waste of time for a priest.*

*I believe such distorted thinking to be the only waste of time. There's nothing left to do but quickly use your brain. You are accustomed to studies, to plans, to pastoral programs, etc. Good. Now make a plan of study for the dutiful task of nourishing yourself in a wholesome, economical, and even enjoyable way. You take care of your car, projectors, and all the things that help in your ministry. Good.*

*Now, take care of yourself, of the food that can help you to be more available to others.*

*How to begin . . . ? Use an outline:*

*a) Make an inventory right away of your cooking equipment; see how many pots, pans, and skillets you have and where they are located. Decide if you wish to leave them where they are or to arrange them in a more logical way.*

*b) See also if you have the electric appliances that can facilitate and speed up your work. If you don't have any because the housekeeper was accustomed to doing things as people did 100 years ago, remedy the situation. There are electric appliances that are easy to operate and clean. Seek advice from those who know about them, not because they sell them, but because they use them!*

*A good electric appliance is a great help.*

*c) Make an inventory of necessary goods: pasta, rice, coffee, tea, sugar, salt, oil, vinegar, butter, milk, flour, semolina, wine, bottled water, etc. It is best to have these things on hand because the unforeseen can happen. Such things keep well; therefore, you need buy them only once in a while. You know, or will now learn, that there is daily shopping, i.e., for bread, fruit, vegetables, and milk; and weekly or monthly shopping, i.e., for pasta, rice, oil, salt, etc. If you think about it you will understand very well.*

### Some Principles of a Healthy Diet

Why must we eat? Simple: to restore to the body the substances that are used to keep us alive, to give us energy, and to help us to better carry out our mission.

What are the most important foods? All are important provided they are consumed in an intelligent way.

The healthiest diet is one that is variable, one made up of all the principal foods.

Let's take a look at each type of food:

MEAT is important because it contains protein that serves to reconstruct human tissue. It is better to eat little meat in various ways, that is, not only beef or veal but also lamb, goat, rabbit, pork, etc. But meat contains certain unique important nutrients. It is good to eat all the parts of the animal: roasts, stews, liver, brains; each part has its own different nutritive value. Still, the person who eats *little meat* lives longer and better.

FISH are very important, wholesome, and easy to digest. Not only trout, cod, or salmon, but all fish contain phosphorus and important proteins.

CHEESE AND DAIRY PRODUCTS are very important and rich in proteins and minerals. Here, too, variety is necessary. They are not as harmful as meat and have fewer contraindications.

VEGETABLES AND FRUITS should always be eaten in abundance, according to the season, and raw, if possible, because their nutritive value is greatly changed by cooking. Fruit and vegetables assure the body of vitamins, minerals, and water. Water is important to maintain the body's constant temperature and helps in the assimilation of foods.

CURED MEATS AND CANNED FOODS are better used rarely, especially because of the preservatives they contain, with the exception of homemade cured meats or those professionally made.

CONDIMENTS such as oil and butter are better if eaten raw. However, it is even better to use very few condiments.

## What Hurts You?

Except in certain cases, what hurts you is that which is eaten reluctantly or not well made. It's unlikely that something you like will harm you.

The body has exceptional defense mechanisms, and there is good harmony between our various "systems." If the good smell of food or the fine look of it is registered in our brain, the brain "telephones" the stomach informing it of what was seen. The stomach happily responds making the mouth water, which is nothing more than an OK to accept the food smelled or seen. Many things are not digested for reasons of uneasiness or tension. Cooking is an excellent therapy.

## How Can a Meal Be Put Together?

Easy: with foods that contain all the important nutrients.

Usually a first course is served: soup, pasta or rice (which contain starches and sugar), vegetables, and fruit.

When pasta is eaten, meat should not be eaten, only cheese and vegetables.

Pay attention to the combinations: pasta is quickly digested, so is meat alone, but pasta and meat together complicate life.

Be careful, also, of getting enough vitamins: raw vegetables guarantee them. As for fruit, except for apples, they should always be eaten outside of meals.

Some simple recipes, surely, to start. Then other recipes that you can find in the other chapters; that which is closest to your situation is "husband alone, wife on vacation."

I give the ingredients for 2 servings, not because you should eat for 2, but because if you want to invite someone it's easier for you to make the portions. I'm confident since you know math!

★          ★          ★

## NOODLES WITH BUTTER AND SAGE

*Ingredients for 2 servings:*

**7 oz. fresh noodles or 6 oz. dry egg noodles**
**2 tablespoons butter**
**1 tablespoon salt**
**1 sprig sage**
**2 tablespoons Parmesan cheese**

Take a large pot (a tall one—saucepans are lower; skillets are the lowest and have only one handle) and in it put a quart of hot water, add salt and bring to a boil (cover large pots with a lid so the water boils faster and you use less gas or electricity).

When the water boils add the noodles and stir well so you're not left with tangled noodles; you must separate the noodles from one another. While the noodles cook (5 minutes for fresh pasta, and 15 minutes for dry pasta) in a small pot heat the butter and the washed sage; let them brown, not burn. Drain the pasta and season with butter and sage and Parmesan.

• This dish is good and light; it's beneficial because the sage is medicinal.

## SPAGHETTI WITH GORGONZOLA

*Ingredients for 2 servings:*

**6 oz. spaghetti**
**4 oz. gorgonzola cheese**
**2 tablespoons butter**
**2 tablespoons Parmesan**
**1 tablespoon salt**

Heat a covered pot with 1 quart of salted water to boiling.

While the water heats, cut the gorgonzola in pieces and grate the Parmesan. When the water boils add a tablespoon of oil and throw in the spaghetti. Boil for the amount of time indicated on the package.

Drain the spaghetti while putting the butter and gorgonzola in the pot. Return the spaghetti to the pot with the butter and gorgonzola and heat for about 1 minute, stirring slowly. Turn off the heat and add the Parmesan, stir again, and "Buon Appetito."

• This dish is good, nutritious, and tasty. To complete it all that's needed is a good mixed salad or seasonal fresh fruit. Nothing else is necessary.

You can season potato gnocchi and polenta in this manner, also.

★   ★   ★

## MUSHROOM RISOTTO

*Ingredients for 2 servings:*

**6 oz. rice**
**2 tablespoons butter**
**1 small onion**
**1 sprig sage**
**1 sprig rosemary**
**1 package dried mushrooms**
**½ teaspoon salt**
**½ glass white wine**
**1 tablespoon oil**

Wash and finely chop the onion. Put the oil in a pan and sauté the onion over low heat.

While the onion is cooking, heat to boiling a small pot with 2 cups of water, salt, sage, and rosemary. When the onion is a golden color add the rice to the pan, stir well, and add ½ glass of dry white wine.

Stirring, let the wine evaporate and add half the herbed broth (the boiling water with the sage and rosemary) previously prepared. Continue cooking, stirring occasionally.

In the meantime, put the dried mushrooms in a cup and cover them with a ladleful of herbed broth previously prepared; leave them in the broth 2 or 3 minutes, then pour the broth into the pan. Meanwhile if the rice has absorbed all the broth, add more and stir.

Then chop the softened mushrooms, add them to the rice, and continue stirring.

When the rice is almost cooked, add the butter and Parmesan, stirring constantly.

- This is an excellent risotto.

## PASTINA IN BROTH

*Ingredients for 2 servings:*

2  **soup plates beef broth**
2  **heaping tablespoons pastina (for a thin soup)**
   **or**
4  **heaping tablespoons (for a thicker soup)**
2  **tablespoons Parmesan cheese**

Heat the beef broth in a small pot. When it boils add the pastina, stir, and cook for 15 minutes. When the cooking is finished add the Parmesan, and the soup is ready.

- You'll find other soups in chapters 1 and 3.

## BOILED BEEF

*Ingredients for 2 servings:*

**14 oz. round, ribs or shoulder meat**
**1 beef bone**
**1 carrot**
**1 rib celery**
**1 onion**
**1 tomato**
**1 sprig sage**
**1 sprig rosemary**
**1 tablespoon salt**

Wash and chop the vegetables and herbs, combine them in a pot with enough water to cover the meat later, and bring to a boil.

Now add the meat and bones (wash the bones well). Cover and cook over a minimum heat for at least 2 hours. Careful! It's important to add the meat to the pot only when the water is boiling; this way it remains tastier. If you add the meat to the cold water instead, the nutrients pass into the soup: you'll have an excellent broth but poor meat.

After about 2 hours when the meat is cooked, put it in a dish; you can eat it as is or you can accompany it with sauces, such as mayonnaise, tuna, mustard, or catsup.

● The boiled meat is also good seasoned with oil, salt, pepper, and maybe some onion. The broth from the boiled meat can be saved for soups or even used for risotto.

★        ★        ★

## RABBIT WITH POTATOES

*Ingredients for 2 servings:*

**4 pieces rabbit about 4 oz. each**
**1 sprig rosemary**
**1 leaf laurel**
**7 oz. fresh or peeled tomatoes**
**½ glass white wine**
**2 tablespoons olive oil**
**7 oz. potatoes**

Wash the rosemary and laurel, put them in a saucepan with the oil, and heat. When the oil is hot add the rabbit and brown the pieces on all sides, adding salt.

Then add the white wine and let it evaporate, also adding the fresh tomatoes (washed and cut into thin slices) or the peeled tomatoes.

Cover and cook over low heat for 5 minutes.

Meanwhile, peel and wash the potatoes, cut into pieces, add them to the rabbit, and mix well. Continue cooking for 20 minutes.

When it's done, add salt to the potatoes and mix. It's ready.

• This is a single, complete dish. When you take the trouble to make a dish such as this one, it's worthwhile to prepare more portions so you'll have them ready for another day.

★     ★     ★

## WHITING WITH BUTTER

*Ingredients for 2 servings:*

**2 pieces of fish about 8 oz. (whiting, swordfish, or
    tuna)**
**2 tablespoons butter**
**1 sprig sage**
    **salt**

Combine the butter and sage in a skillet, melt the butter, add the fish, and brown over high heat turning the fish occasionally with a fork to avoid breaking it.

Sprinkle both sides of the fish with salt.

Six minutes cooking time is enough . . . and the fish is ready.

● Fish made like this is good, and you can accompany it with a fine salad.

★        ★        ★

## ROASTED PEPPERS

*Ingredients for 2 servings:*

**4 large and meaty peppers (about 2 lbs.)**
**2 tablespoons olive oil**
    **salt**
    **vinegar**

Take a baking dish and line it with aluminum foil. Wash and dry the peppers and lay them on the foil. Preheat the oven to 475°, bake the peppers for 15 minutes, then turn the peppers and let them brown well on all sides (it will take about an hour).

When they're done, turn off the oven but leave them inside for 10 minutes.

Remove the peppers from the baking dish and put them in a nylon bag to cool. When they have cooled take them out of the bag and peel them; it will be easy.

Remove the seeds and put the cleaned and cooked peppers in a bowl seasoning them with oil, salt, and then vinegar. Mix well.

● They're tasty; you can eat them like this or with anchovies. They go well with boiled beef, grilled meat, and even fish.

★          ★          ★

## STIMULATING POTATOES

*Ingredients for 2 servings:*

10½ oz. potatoes
1 small bunch parsley
1 tablespoon capers
4 tablespoons olive oil
1 tablespoon vinegar
  anchovies
  mustard
  salt

Put the potatoes, unpeeled, in a pot, cover with cold water, and bring to a boil.

When the water starts boiling, cook for 20 minutes. Let the potatoes cool and in the meantime wash and mince the parsley together with the anchovies and capers. Put this chopped mixture in a bowl and season with oil, salt, pepper, and mustard; mix well. Now peel the potatoes and cube or slice them; season with a little oil and salt and mix well. Add the prepared sauce and . . . they're ready!

● As I've already said you'll find other recipes in various other chapters or in the Index at the end of the book.

# 5

# WHEN CHILDREN HAVE NO APPETITE

*1. Examine the cause. Often it's psychological. When this is so the difficulties increase putting the parents' psychological cleverness to a tough test: conflicts among married couples, prolonged absences, nervousness and exhaustion taken out on the children, etc.*

*2. Once the cause has been established, if it is not of a medical nature the remedy is simpler. The pediatrician will give you the diet. If the cause is psychological, things are challenging but can be remedied. Prepare foods that the children will eat more willingly. Do it calmly without an anxious presentation, useless pleas, promises. What are needed are appetizing, nutritious, wholesome dishes.*

*All this must be combined with a search for the true causes. It is very useful to involve the children in the preparation of foods, making them play at home. Every one of you, if willing, knows how to resolve the problem—provided you not set a price that you expect to pay. Children have a right to a peaceful life; therefore, your problems must not be passed on to them.*

*Children feel what you think as well as what you say. As far as you are concerned, remember that children always know how to give back, at least at this age, what they receive. A happy child is a friend of yours for life!*

★     ★     ★

**SWEET SEMOLINA WITH EGG**

*Ingredients for 2 servings:*

**1 qt. milk**
**2 tablespoons semolina**
**1 pinch salt**
**2 tablespoons sugar**
**2 eggs**

Combine the milk and salt in a pot. Heat to boiling. When it boils add the semolina bit by bit, mixing well to avoid lumps.

When all the semolina has been added, cook for at least 15 minutes stirring constantly. After 15 minutes turn off the heat, immediately add 2 egg yolks, and mix vigorously to blend them with the semolina. Finally, add the sugar and mix. It's ready.

• This is a wholesome and nutritious dish. The semolina is obtained from wheat and is the external part of the shell of the grain: the richest in protein; the milk is nutritious and the raw egg yolks are easier to digest. The sugar completes the diet picture. This can truly be a complete meal; children like it because it's sweet, creamy, and easy to chew.

To complete the menu all you need to add is some good and ripe fresh fruit.

★　　★　　★

## PASTA WITH PARMESAN AND OIL

*Ingredients for 2 servings:*

**3½ oz. pasta (whatever the child likes)**
 **2 tablespoons olive oil**
 **2 tablespoons Parmesan cheese**
  **salt**

Heat a quart of water in a pot and add a tablespoon of salt.

When the water boils add the pasta, stir, and cook for 15 minutes. Drain the pasta and season with raw oil and Parmesan.

• This is a simple and good first course.

It is important to choose pasta made from durum wheat.

★　　★　　★

## POTATO GNOCCHI WITH TOMATOES AND MOZZARELLA

*Ingredients for 2 servings:*

**4 oz. fresh gnocchi**
**2 oz. fresh or frozen peas (never canned)**
**2 slices prosciutto, lean and without preservatives**
**2 tablespoons olive oil**
**2 tablespoons Parmesan cheese**
  **salt**

Bring to a boil a pot with 1 quart of salted water.

When the water boils throw in the gnocchi, leave the pot uncovered, and wait till the gnocchi, boiling, float to the top, then boil for 2 or 3 minutes.

Remove the gnocchi with a slotted spoon draining well. Put them in a plate alternating gnocchi, raw tomatoes or ground peeled tomatoes, oil, Parmesan, and diced mozzarella. Cover the dish for a moment so that the mozzarella melts and it's ready.

• This can be considered a nutritious and complete meal. Using raw tomatoes retains the vitamins. If you use peeled tomatoes it's best to prepare a good fruit whip or some fresh fruit of your choice.

*Note:* You can buy the gnocchi at a reliable pasta factory. If you want to prepare them at home look for the recipe in the Index of this book.

★　　　★　　　★

## SPINACH GNOCCHI

*Ingredients for 2 servings:*

4 oz. boiled spinach
2 oz. ricotta cheese
2 egg yolks
2 tablespoons Parmesan cheese
1 tablespoon flour
  *To season:*
2 tablespoons butter
2 tablespoons Parmesan cheese
  salt

Squeeze the boiled spinach and place it in a blender, blend for a second, then add the ricotta, egg yolks, flour, and Parmesan. Blend; the mixture should be thick and smooth.

Take a pot (a large, low-sided one is best), fill with 1 quart of water and 1 tablespoon of salt, and heat. When the water boils take a teaspoonful of dough and with the aid of another spoon drop the dough into the boiling water.

Don't worry about the gnocchi floating to the surface. When you have used up all the dough, heat to boilding and wait for all the gnocchi to float to the surface, then quickly remove them with a slotted spoon.

Melt the butter in a small pan (just melt it, don't let it fry because fried fat is not good for children—their livers are more delicate than ours). Season with the melted butter and the Parmesan.

• The ricotta is wholesome, the spinach contains iron, the eggs are a complete food, the butter and Parmesan make it a lordly dish that is certainly not lacking in nutritious value!

## PIZZA WITH FRESH TOMATOES

*Ingredients for 2 servings:*

**14 oz. bread dough, already made**
**7 oz. fresh or homemade peeled tomatoes**
**3½ oz. mozzarella cheese**
**1 tablespoon oil**
**1 pinch oregano**
    **salt**

Children love pizza. However, it's worth making at home. If you have difficulty making the dough, you can remedy that by buying bread dough, already made, from the baker, raw, of course, already risen and ready to roll out, season, and cook.

Roll out the dough no thicker than ¾".

Grease the pizza pan with a bit of olive oil and lay the rolled out dough on it; season with fresh chopped tomatoes or crushed peeled tomatoes, sliced mozzarella, oil, and oregano. Bake in a hot oven 475° for 30 minutes.

• Even this can be a complete meal. If the child eats a good slice of homemade pizza you can consider him or her nourished. Fresh fruit eaten as is or as squeezed juice, or fruit sherbert should never be missing.

★          ★          ★

## RICE AND CHEESE

*Ingredients for 2 servings:*

7  oz. rice
4  oz. various cheeses (1 oz. mozzarella, 1 oz. strac-
     chino, 1 oz. Bel Paese, 1 oz. Parmesan)
2  teaspoons olive oil
    salt

*Note:* Don't use fatty or piquant cheeses or packaged cheese slices since these are usually made from by-products.

Children usually love cheese. Making a game of hiding the cheese in the rice can be a good and wholesome idea. You can also have a contest to see who will find the various kinds of cheeses in the rice. The child will have fun and, above all, will be well nourished because the cheese is rich in protein and minerals, exactly what's needed to insure a consistent physical growth.

Bring a pot with 1 quart of salted water to boiling. When the water boils add the rice, stir well, and let the rice boil, uncovered, for 20 minutes.

Drain and place the assorted diced cheeses in the pot where the rice was cooked; heat for a moment over minimum heat to melt the cheese. Turn off the heat and add the Parmesan. It's ready.

• This is a super-complete dish, nutritious and easy to digest. Complete the meal with fresh fruit.

★     ★     ★

## SPAGHETTI WITH TOMATO SAUCE

*Ingredients for 2 servings:*

**4 oz. thin spaghetti**
**3½ oz. very ripe tomatoes**
**1 sprig basil**
**1 small onion**
**1 small bunch parsley**
**2 teaspoons extra-virgin olive oil**
**2 tablespoons Parmesan cheese**
   **salt**

Wash the tomatoes well. In a small saucepan combine the tomatoes, the onion, parsley, and basil, then add 1 teaspoon of salt. Cover the pan and cook for 10 minutes.

While the tomatoes are cooking heat a pot with 2 cups of water and a pinch of salt; when the water boils throw in the spaghetti and stir immediately to separate them well.

Cook for 7 or 8 minutes. Meanwhile, pass the tomatoes and herbs through a vegetable press or grinder, gathering the sauce in a bowl. Drain the spaghetti and season with the sauce, oil, and Parmesan.

• This is light and tasty spaghetti. It stimulates children who love tomato sauce. It is not advisable to buy prepared sauces because they have too many preservatives.

★          ★          ★

## NOODLES WITH PEAS AND PROSCIUTTO

*Ingredients for 2 servings:*

**4 oz. fresh noodles**
**2 oz. fresh or frozen peas (never canned)**
**2 slices lean prosciutto without preservatives**
**2 tablespoons olive oil**
**2 tablespoons Parmesan cheese**
   **salt**

Put 1 tablespoon of oil in a small saucepan; add the shelled or frozen peas and a pinch of salt. Cover the pan and cook over low heat for 25-30 minutes.

Add ½ glass of cold water if the peas start to burn. On a cutting board roll the 2 slices of prosciutto together and cut them into strips; then add them to the peas and turn off the heat.

Bring to a boil a quart of salted water. When the water boils throw in the noodles and let them cook for 5 or 7 minutes. Drain and season with the peas, prosciutto, olive oil, and Parmesan cheese.

• This is an excellent dish. You can complete the meal with some fresh fruit.

★   ★   ★

## VEAL AND SPINACH PATTIES

*Ingredients for 2 servings:*

4 oz. ground veal
2 slices prosciutto
1 egg
1 tablespoon olive oil
4 oz. boiled spinach
  salt

Buy 4 oz. of veal (from the leg) and 2 slices of prosciutto from the butcher and have him grind them up together.

At home make the patties like this: take the meat, prosciutto, the boiled spinach (which has been passed through a vegetable grinder), an egg, and a pinch of salt; mix it all together. Then make 2 balls and flatten them until they are about ¾ inch thick.

In a small frying pan heat 1 tablespoon of oil, add the patties, and brown them for 1 minute on one side and 2 minutes on the other side. They're ready.

• These constitute a single course, tasty and nutritious. Don't forget, however, the fresh fruit or fruit sherbert.

★        ★        ★

## PROSCIUTTO AND MOZZARELLA

*Ingredients for 2 servings:*

**2 oz. prosciutto**
**2 oz. mozzarella**

Take 2 slices of prosciutto and lay them on the cutting board, then cut the mozzarella into thin sticks (like French fries). Put half the mozzarella on one slice of prosciutto and the rest of the mozzarella on the other. Roll up the prosciutto and the dish is ready.

• This is a nutritious main course but, at the same time, a light, suitable accompaniment to a first course of spaghetti or vegetable soup. In this case, also, fresh fruit shouldn't be lacking.

★        ★        ★

## EGGS AND FRENCH FRIES

*Ingredients for 2 servings:*

**2 fresh eggs**
**4 oz. potatoes**
**2 glasses extra-virgin olive oil**
  **salt**

Peel the potatoes, wash and dry them, and cut them into sticks.

Heat the olive oil in a frying pan and add the potatoes, cooking them to a golden color. *Note:* It is never necessary to torment the potatoes by poking them with a fork. They are done when they float to the surface, light and golden.

When they're ready remove them with a slotted spoon to a plate lined with a paper towel. Add salt. Then put 2 eggs in a small pot, cover with cold water, and bring to a boil. They don't need to boil for more than 1 minute.

The eggs are then put into egg cups, the ends opened and sprinkled with salt. Arrange the potatoes around them so that the children can enjoy themselves by dipping them in the egg.

★          ★          ★

## MASHED POTATOES WITH EGGS

*Ingredients for 2 servings:*

5  oz. potatoes
2  fresh eggs
2  tablespoons butter
2  tablespoons Parmesan cheese
4  tablespoons milk
   salt

Peel the potatoes, wash them and cook them in cold water with a pinch of salt; let them boil for 20 minutes. Remove from heat and mash.

Add the milk, stir vigorously, and heat the puree; then add the butter, Parmesan, and the 2 eggs. Mix again and serve hot. If you must wait to eat, keep it hot in the oven or a double boiler.

Don't heat this mixture directly over the heat because you may alter the taste and you may overcook the eggs, which must remain raw so that they are easier to digest and give more taste to the dish.

• This is a simple recipe to make but very important for the nutritive value it contains. To complete the menu fresh seasonal fruit is all that's needed.

★          ★          ★

## CALF LIVER AND PEAS

*Ingredients for 2 servings:*

**5 oz. calf liver**
**3½ oz. fresh or frozen peas**
**2 tablespoons butter**
**2 leaves sage**
**salt**

Put the butter and sage in a small saucepan, add the peas, sauté a couple of minutes, add ½ glass of water, and cover.

Cook over minimum heat for 15 minutes, then remove the lid and let the remaining water evaporate.

Cut the liver into strips, add it to the peas, let it brown, and salt it; it must cook 2 or 3 minutes and it's ready.

• This is a nutritious, wholesome, and complete dish. To get children to eat it you can tell this story: there were some shy peas who were afraid to be alone, but then the liver arrived, strong, rich in iron and potent vitamins, and the peas felt more secure. So, too, all those who eat peas and liver will become strong and courageous.

★          ★          ★

## BREAD STICKS AND PROSCIUTTO

*Ingredients for 2 servings:*

**3½ oz. prosciutto**
**2 oz. well-cooked bread sticks**

Put the bread sticks in a glass. Cut the prosciutto into strips and arrange them on a plate. Each child must take a bread stick, cover it with a strip of prosciutto, and eat it. The winner is the one who eats the most covered bread sticks.

• The children have fun but also feed themselves in a wholesome way because the prosciutto contains protein and the bread sticks are rich in sugar and, therefore, energizing.

It's advisable to choose natural bread sticks, not seasoned ones, that is, those made simply from bread dough.

**POTATO AND PROSCIUTTO PIE**

*Ingredients for 2 servings:*

5 oz. potatoes
3½ oz. cooked prosciutto
2 tablespoons butter
2 tablespoons Parmesan cheese
2 tablespoons milk
1 egg
  salt

Prepare mashed potatoes (*see the recipe on page 93*), add an egg to this, beat the mixture well, then take a pie pan, grease it with a little butter, put half the potato mixture in it, lay the slices of prosciutto over the potatoes, and top with the remaining potatoes.

Light the oven to 475° and bake the pie. It's done when it turns golden (usually about 15 minutes).

• This is a complete dish in itself. The idea of eating a salty pie is enjoyable to children and to their parents!

★      ★      ★

## MIXED MEAT MEDALLIONS

*Ingredients for 2 servings:*

3 oz. veal
3 oz. prosciutto
3 oz. chicken breast
1 egg
2 tablespoons Parmesan cheese
1 small bunch parsley, chopped
   the crumbs from half a roll
   milk
   salt
*For the sauce:*
1 tablespoon butter
1 tablespoon flour
3 oz. grated Gruyere cheese
1 glass milk
   salt

With a meat grinder grind the chicken, veal, and prosciutto. Put the ground meat in a bowl, add the egg, parsley, Parmesan, and the bread crumbs soaked in the milk. Blend everything together into a smooth and moist mixture.

Make 2 or 4 round meatballs and flatten slightly. Now put the medallions in a deep dish, cover them with another dish, and steam them for 20 minutes on one side and 20 minutes on the other.

While the medallions are cooking prepare the sauce like this: melt the butter in a small pot, add the flour stirring well to smooth out the lumps, and little by little add the Gruyere and the milk, stirring constantly. Cook this creamy mixture for 15 minutes, then pour it on the steamed medallions.

● This is a very tasty and nutritious dish; complete the menu with a fine salad of raw carrots seasoned with salt, oil, and lemon juice. There's no need for fruit since there are vitamins in the carrots and lemon juice, while the meat and cheese contain protein.

★     ★     ★

## TRI-COLOR RICE

*Ingredients for 2 servings:*

**4 tablespoons rice**
**2 oz. string beans**
**2 carrots**
**2 tablespoons Parmesan cheese**
**2 hard-boiled egg yolks**
**2 tablespoons butter**
   **salt**

Wash and chop the beans and carrots. Heat a pot with 2 cups of water, a little salt, and the carrots to boiling. When the water boils add the beans and cook for 10 minutes. Then throw in the rice and cook it together with the vegetables, stirring occasionally.

When the rice is cooked turn off the heat and add the butter and Parmesan. Stir, cover, and leave it covered for 1 minute. Form the rice into a little mound and sprinkle with the grated egg yolk.

● The happy colors of this dish will stimulate the children's appetites, and it is a wholesome, nutritious, and complete meal. All that's needed is some good fresh fruit.

★     ★     ★

## SPINACH SOUP

*Ingredients for 2 servings:*

**4 thin slices of bread**
**4 oz. milk**
**2 tablespoons Parmesan cheese**
**8 spinach leaves**
**2 teaspoons extra-virgin olive oil**
**1 pinch salt**

Wash the spinach well, chop it, and put it in a pot with salt and the milk.

Cook over low heat for 15 minutes, remove from heat, add the Parmesan and oil to the spinach, and then mix.

In each dish put 2 slices of bread cut into pieces and pour the mixture on top; let it rest for 5 minutes and mix again. It's ready.

● This soup is good and nutritious as well as an intelligent way to make a child eat stale bread and spinach. Jokingly this dish can be called "Popeye makes friends with the baker."

## ZUCCHINI TRAIN

*Ingredients for 2 servings:*

**2 fresh zucchini**
**1 tablespoon melted butter**
**2 tablespoons mashed potatoes**
**2 tablespoons Parmesan cheese**
**2 tablespoons milk**
**1 pinch chopped parsley**
  **salt**

Heat a small amount of salted water to boiling. When the water boils add the zucchini (cleaned and washed). Cook for 15 minutes, then cool them under running water and cut them in half length-wise. Scoop out the inside of the zucchini with a spoon forming 4 boats.

Finely chop the scooped out zucchini and add the potatoes and chopped parsley to this; blend together.

Fill the zucchini with this mixture, putting on top of each a little melted butter and a pinch of Parmesan. Put 2 tablespoons of milk in a baking dish, cut each zucchini into 3 equal parts, and arrange them to resemble the wagons of a train. Cook in a hot oven at 400° for 15 minutes.

When serving the vegetable to the children, transfer the pieces of zucchini to a plate connecting the pieces with a wooden toothpick to make a little green train! This unusual presentation intrigues the child who, as the good engineer, will be tempted to eat the train (it is to be hoped that he'll not want to save it as a toy).

# 6

# WHEN YOU FORGET TO DO
# THE SHOPPING

*"Necessity is the mother of invention."*

*What counts in every circumstance is to be optimistic, ingenious, and capable of laughing at your own mistakes. Many times I have found myself with an empty pantry and refrigerator and guests at the table. I have devised some remedies that I will offer to you.*

*To avoid these problems it is necessary to "hide" in the house a package of pasta, sugar, a bottle of oil, a can of peas, and tuna.*

*Then in the freezer hide single servings already cooked. I use these things only when it's their turn, that is, for the emergency I envisioned when I saved them, or when I can replace them the same day. If I use them when I don't want to cook or go out, then I really deserve to fast!*

First, let's see what you have in the house:

You have no bread but you have potatoes, butter, pasta, rice, Parmesan; make a potato pie with mashed potatoes, add butter and Parmesan, put it in the oven (bake for 15 minutes in a very hot oven).

You can eat this pie with: a steak with butter;
an egg with butter.

If you have neither meat nor eggs but some cheese, put the cheese in the pie and you'll have a complete course.

If you have only stale bread, potatoes, and a fatty cheese: *make a pizza.*

If you have only pasta to be cooked or already cooked: make a hearty omelet.

If you have only vegetables, for example, 2 potatoes, 1 onion, 1 forgotten, shriveled pepper, 1 tomato or some peeled tomatoes (you're rich!), make an imaginative caponata.

Do you have only rice, assorted cheeses somewhat unpresentable, and maybe a forgotten egg? Stupendous: make rice with Italian cheeses!

You have only 1 piece of meat, 2 potatoes, and 2 eggs? Make an omelet with potatoes, sliced meat, and beaten eggs.

# 7

## WHEN YOU INVITE FRIENDS
## TO THE COUNTRY

*It is curious to see neighbors packing the car with all the necessities for a dinner or maybe supper eaten out in the country. The car is packed with everything: table, chairs, picnic hampers; you would think they were going away for 2 weeks! Then you see them return at night. A picnic dinner should be a sporty meal, nutritious and good; but if you take the kitchen and the dining room with you, you might as well stay home. It should be a meal that permits everyone to have a relaxing time. A single course with some side dishes, assorted rolls, prepared at home and then eaten together without one person having to do the work while the rest of the family are eating.*

*An even more enjoyable way is to take the main ingredients—bread and assorted fillings—and each person puts together his or her own meal on the spot, joyously celebrating the holiday and the trip together.*

*We all long for barbecues (stupendous). Bring the barbecue victims marinating in a sealed container. A barbecue grill, bread, and wine. Around the fire it's always a festive occasion.*

*Go to the country only if you have the courage to confront nature where all is silent, orderly, and peaceful.*

*If you're in a bad mood you risk being out of tune much more than staying at home.*

## RICE SALAD

*Ingredients:*

**2 oz. rice per person (rice for the salad)**
   **carrots**
   **celery**
   **tomatoes**
   **peppers**
   **boiled beans (in jars)**
   **boiled peas**
   **pickles**
   **hard-boiled eggs**
   **tuna**
   **olives**
   **frankfurters**
   **cheeses (fontina, berna, asiago)**
   **parsley**
   **catsup**
   **oil**
   **vinegar**
   **salt**
   *The amounts of vegetables, washed and chopped, are calculated in pinches.*
   *For the peas and beans: 1 tablespoon per person.*
   *For the tuna and the cheese: 1 oz. per person.*

Let me quickly say that this is a very rich rice dish, but it's also a complete meal for a country hunger.

Bring to a boil a pot with hot sealed water. When the water boils add the rice, stir, and cook, uncovered, for the amount of time indicated on the package.

Drain the rice, quickly put it under running water to cool it, and rinse out the starch. Wash and chop the vegetables. Also chop the frankfurters and hard-boiled eggs, the cheese and the pickles.

Open up the jars of peas and beans and drain them. Put the rice in a container big enough to hold all the ingredients you have decided to add (except the parsley and catsup), vegetables, cured meats, and cheese.

Season with pepper, salt, oil, and vinegar and mix well. At this point divide the rice into 3 parts.

Leave one part as is; to the second add 2 tablespoons of catsup and mix.

To the third add chopped parsley. This way you have 3 kinds of salad.

• A few things are enough to create various dishes with different tastes to confront one's appetite on a trip. This can truly be a complete meal—in fact, it contains all the principal foods needed for healthy and light nourishment.

★        ★        ★

## HOMEMADE SANDWICHES

Sandwiches eaten in the country should be nutritious and easy to digest, while not making one thirsty.

### Rolls with Zucchini and Hard-boiled Eggs

**2 or 3 pieces of zucchini with vinegar
some slices of hard-boiled eggs**

Cut the roll in half or cut the bread in slices. Put the zucchini on one side and add 2 or 3 slices of egg.

Top with the other piece of bread. Wrap each roll in aluminum foil.

• You'll have a tasty, soft, thirst-quenching sandwich.

## Rolls with Roasted Peppers and Anchovies

**2 or 3 pieces peeled, roasted peppers**
**2 anchovy fillets.**

Cut the bread, and on one piece put some slices of roasted pepper that have been seasoned with salt, oil, and vinegar.

Also add 2 anchovy fillets. Top with the other half of the roll and wrap in aluminum foil.

_____

## Rolls with Chicory and Eggs

**1 tablespoon chicory cut into strips and seasoned as you prefer**
**2 or 4 slices of hard-boiled eggs**

Prepare the chicory washing it and thinly slicing it.

Season the salad. Put 1 tablespoon of chicory on one piece of bread and add the eggs. Top with another piece of bread. Wrap in aluminum foil.

● It's appetizing, thirst-quenching, and healthy.

_____

## Rolls with Tomato, Mozzarella, and Oregano

**2 slices tomato**
**2 slices mozzarella**
**1 pinch oregano**

Wash and slice the tomatoes. Season them with salt, oil, and vinegar, then mix.

Also slice the mozzarella and season it with oregano, oil, and vinegar.

Cut the roll and place 2 slices of tomato and 2 slices of mozzarella on one side. Top with the other half of the roll and wrap in aluminum foil.

● It is thirst-quenching and very soft.

_____

### Rolls with Eggs and Bacon

    1  egg
    2  slices smoked bacon
       a little butter

Melt the butter in a skillet, then add the eggs, cook them on both sides, and add a little salt.

Put 2 slices of bacon over each egg, cover the pan, and cook for 1 minute. Cool.

Cut the bread; in each roll put one egg with the bacon, put the other half of the roll on top, and wrap in aluminum foil.

● You'll have a different and tasty sandwich, but less thirst-quenching than the others.

★          ★          ★

### BARBECUED DINNER

If you want to barbecue, it is necessary to prepare the various marinated meats at home. It is useful to bring some sauce to accompany the roasted meats.

For example: some catsup, green sauce, horseradish, or simply a jar containing a mixture of: oil, pepper, salt, and chopped basil. Beat these together and put them in a closed jar.

    Suitable Meats: pork chops: 1 each
                    veal chops: 1 each
                    rabbit fillet: 7 oz. each
                    chicken or turkey cutlet: 1 each
                    sausage: 4 oz. each

MARINATE: In a container with a tight-fitting lid put a layer of the selected meat, add a little pepper, salt, oil, and rosemary, and it's ready. The sausage doesn't need marinating: it's fine the way it is.

Cover the container and keep it in the refrigerator all night. Don't forget it, however, in the refrigerator!

When you're ready to cook the meat, put it on the barbecue grill over the coals and cook over low heat for a few minutes on each side. The sausage is put as is on the grill.

★　　　★　　　★

## KABOBS

Kabobs can be made with the meats indicated for the barbarcue. They simply have to be cut into chunks rather than slices. Kabobs can be made with a single type of meat or with assorted types.

★　　　★　　　★

## FANTASTIC KABOBS

*Ingredients for 1 serving:*

  2 oz. pork
  2 oz. veal
  2 oz. sausage
  2 oz. chicken breast
 10 leaves sage
  5 slices bacon

Cut the meat into chunks keeping each type of meat separate. Cut each slice of bacon into 4 pieces. Remove the sage leaves; wash and dry them.

Take a wooden or metal skewer, thread a piece of bacon, a sage leaf, a piece of pork, a piece of bacon, a sage leaf, a piece of veal and follow with bacon, sage, sausage, bacon, sage, chicken or turkey, bacon, sage, etc.

Prepare at least 2 kabobs in this way for each person.

If you are using wooden skewers you must cover the grill with aluminum foil and lay it on the coals. When the grill is hot enough set the kabobs on the grill and let them brown uniformly on each side for a few minutes.

Then remove them from the grill, add salt and pepper, and they're ready.

The aluminum foil lets the kabobs cook without the risk of the wooden skewers catching fire. If you use metal skewers there is no need for the aluminum foil: just put the kabobs directly on the grill.

• Barbecued meat is healthy and tasty, the extra fat melts and is lost, and in this way you're spared from eating fats difficult to digest and, therefore, unhealthy.

★          ★          ★

## CHICKEN AND SAGE KABOBS

*Ingredients for 1 serving:*

**7  oz. chicken**
**2  slices lard**
**10  leaves sage**

Clean the chicken, then wash and cut it into pieces: 4 nice pieces for each person. Cut the lard into pieces: 2 pieces for each piece of meat. Remove the sage leaves, wash, and dry them.

Take a wooden or metal skewer. Thread the sage, lard, and the chicken alternating each piece of chicken with the lard and sage. Prepare all the kabobs in this manner and barbecue them for at least 30 minutes.

Remember, you have not only meat here but also bones: the cooking time is longer. When they are cooked add salt and pepper.

• You now have a healthy and very tasty dish, a dish from our ancestors.

★          ★          ★

## MEAT AND VEGETABLE KABOBS

*Ingredients for 1 serving:*

  **5 oz. meat (pork, veal, chicken, sausage)**
  **3½ oz. vegetables (potatoes, carrots, celery, onions,**
     **peppers)**
  **4 slices bacon**
**10 leaves sage**
    **salt**
    **pepper**

Follow the procedure for "Fantastic Kabobs" adding a thick chunk of vegetable between each meat-bacon-sage section and another. Alternate potatoes, carrots, onions, celery, and peppers. Barbecue in the same way, but it's necessary to prolong the cooking time for at least 10 minutes, therefore, 20 minutes in all.

● These kabobs are excellent and complete because you have meat and vegetables. *Important: add salt only after cooking.*

## MAKING SANDWICHES AT THE PICNIC GROUNDS

It's pleasant working together and enjoyable besides to make up a sandwich suited to your own tastes.

You can do it like this. First prepare the foods at home: roasted peppers, zucchini with vinegar, various omelets, assorted roasted meats, carrot salad, Russian salad.

Everything prepared is put into the refrigerator. You can also buy pickles, cold cuts, fresh cheese, frankfurters, etc. Prepare the bread, wine, and soft drinks and don't forget the fruit!

In the morning take the prepared foods in an insulated bag. It is also advisable to take some forks, spoons, knives, and glasses.

When it's time to eat spread out all the food, buffet-style. Each person takes bread or rolls and makes the sandwich of his or her choice.

● This is a practical and lively way to eat; it unites the family in a day of joy and fun and, above all, permits the "lady of the house" to relax, enjoying a different kind of day.

# 8

## AVOIDING MID-MORNING SNACKS

*I often find myself in public places at about 10:00 A.M. I see the usual spectacle: empty desks, waiters coming and going with trays of rolls, pies, donuts, and toast. An office looks like an emergency room for those "dying of hunger."*

*It is the same story in the cafes near the offices. Cafes full of people with drawn faces and languid eyes, purses opening and closing, forced to pay absurd amounts for moderate things.*

*I have always asked myself: don't these people have a home? Don't they have to work 8 hours? Do they all have an ulcer or are they all nursing?*

*When will we learn that a healthy diet includes the time to digest and lets the stomach as well as the wallet rest? A roll at a coffee shop costs a mininum of 80 cents plus a cup of coffee = $1.60. The same thing at home costs 45 cents at the most.*

*It's healthier to eat a roll at 8:00 A.M. than at 10:00 A.M. Do you put gas in the car when it's empty or when you happen to see a gas station? Why can't you concentrate between 8 and 10? You're in need of gas.*

The void between the hours of 6:00 P.M. and 10:00 A.M. is too long; why then do you eat at 10:00 A.M. and at 1:00 P.M. and then again at 6:00 P.M.?

Treat yourself better and you'll see that life will treat you better.

Eating a good breakfast at home costs less and is healthier.

Give yourself an additional 15 minutes with your family.

## Some Ideas for a Joyful Breakfast

| Drinks | Breakfast Foods |
|---|---|
| tea | soft-boiled egg and bread sticks<br>roll with egg and bacon<br>roll with robiola de bec and anchovy paste<br>roll with mozzarella and tomato |
| coffee or<br>cappuccino | apple cake<br>plumcake<br>homemade cookies<br>peaches in syrup |
| hot chocolate | toast<br>bread with butter and jelly<br>bread with butter and honey<br>bread with butter and sugar |
| cappuccino | baked apple<br>baked peaches<br>eggs and fresh bread<br>figs and fresh bread |
| white wine<br>(with rolls it's<br>healthier) | roll with Parmesan cheese and coppa<br>roll with tomato and capers<br>roll with butter and anchovies<br>roll with fontina cheese and prosciutto |

# 9

## WHEN YOUR SALARY DWINDLES
## (AT THE END OF THE MONTH)

*Many people often have difficulty making ends meet at the end of the month because the cost of living rises in such a dizzying way. Don't be distressed, because that makes it difficult to take preventive measures. Take it as an occasion to learn to make new recipes that for years have enabled many people to live calmly and healthily. Don't feel like victims. On the contrary, I advise you to endure this period silently. Enrich the dishes this "week" with joy, like someone who is doing something new or beautiful.*

*Present each dish as a discovery, your secret invention. Talk about it only afterward. At the end of the week don't run to the scale to see how much weight you've lost. Instead, run to the mirror to see how beautiful and relaxed you are. Your energy, too, will be renewed as when you take up again a forgotten exercise.*

*I propose a single course where everything is planned and where neither the principal food nor the principal nutrients are lacking. The proposed recipes will allow you more time at the table and will let you use up forgotten resources with the advantage of replacing the provisions.*

*Some important advice! As soon as you receive your salary replace the provisions: oil, pasta, sugar, and things that can be precious in the "lean days."*

*Joy and economy = health and savings.*

## SPAGHETTI WITH OIL AND ROSEMARY

*Ingredients for 2 servings:*

**7 oz. spaghetti (in this case it's good to prepare a substantial serving of pasta to feel full)**
**4 tablespoons olive oil**
**2 teaspoons salt**
**1 sprig rosemary**

Heat to boiling a pot with 1 quart of water and 1 teaspoon of salt.

When the water boils throw in the spaghetti, stir, and cook for the amount of time indicated on the package. While the spaghetti is cooking put the oil, rosemary, and 1 teaspoon of salt in a small pan.

Fry over low heat for 3 minutes. Drain the pasta and season with the oil, rosemary, and salt.

● This dish is good, healthy, and light as well as tasty.

## PASTA WITH ARUGOLA

*Ingredients for 2 servings:*

**5 oz. fresh pasta**
**1 bunch fresh arugola**
**2 oz. mozzarella cheese**
**2 tablespoons butter or extra-virgin olive oil**
**2 tablespoons Parmesan cheese**

Heat the water and add salt. While waiting for the water to boil, clean and wash the arugola and chop it.

When the water boils throw in the arugola and then the fresh pasta. Cook for 5-7 minutes.

Drain (it's worthwhile to save this water: it's rich in nutrients and can be used for soups, risotto, creams). Put

the hot pasta in a bowl where you've put the diced mozzarella. Add the butter or oil and the Parmesan; mix.

● This dish is excellent, digestible, wholesome, and a
complete meal.

It's good to add a raw vegetable salad just to guarantee the presence of the major vitamins and other nutrients.

*Note:* You can also use dry pasta: in this case you
must first cook the pasta for a little and then add the
arugola, or else it will be overcooked. Complete as above.

★          ★          ★

**POLENTA**

*Ingredients for 2 servings:*

**5  oz. corn flour**
**1  qt. water**
   **salt**
   **oil**

Boil the salted water (if possible on a wood-burning
stove). When the water boils add the flour slowly, stirring
constantly until all the flour has been added.

If the flour is fresh it will absorb less water; if aged it
will need more. Judge for yourself if you should put it all
in, or add more or use less. Stir occasionally for at least 20
minutes. Remove from heat (the best is a copper caldron
over a wood-burning fire—but such things are museum
pieces).

Decide how you want to eat it: with fondue, stew,
salami, sausage.

★          ★          ★

## POLENTA WITH PEPPER AND OLIVE OIL

Follow the preceding recipe to prepare the polenta, but to season it use 2 tablespoons extra-virgin olive oil per person plus some ground pepper.

Prepare the polenta. When it's cooked put a portion in each dish and on top of each portion put 2 tablespoons of extra-virgin olive oil and some ground pepper.

● This dish is very tasty and light and can be a whole meal provided that during dinner you can eat an abundant mixed salad or a good fresh fruit salad.

## STALE BREAD PIE

*Ingredients for 2 servings:*

5 oz. stale bread
2 cups broth (bouillon)
½ beef bouillon cube
2 eggs
2 tablespoons Parmesan cheese
3½ oz. American cheese slices or fontina or moz-
    zarella
  salt

Cut the bread into thin slices and toast them in the oven, but don't burn them!

Meanwhile, in a bowl combine the eggs, Parmesan, and 2 pinches of salt. Beat with a fork like an omelet. When the bread is golden brown take it out of the oven.

Butter a round or rectangular pan and place the toasted bread in the pan in a single layer. Pour the broth—which was prepared with 2 cups of water and ½ of a bouillon cube (meat or vegetable)—over the bread.

Slice the cheese and put it over the bread, top it all with the beaten eggs. Put the pan in a hot oven at 475° and bake to a golden color, 15 minutes if the oven is hot, 30 minutes if it's cold.

● This dish serves as a first course. It's excellent, light, easy to digest.

If you have many people, increase the ingredients and make more layers in the same pan. You can also add, if you like, prosciutto, mortadella, or smoked bacon.

After this dish don't serve potatoes, or starches in general—you'll feel too full.

★      ★      ★

## LENTILS WITH OIL AND CHEESE

*Ingredients for 2 servings:*

3 cups lentils
8 cups water
4 tablespoons extra-virgin olive oil
2 heaping tablespoons Parmesan cheese
  salt

Remove the tiny stones that are sometimes found in the lentils. Wash them under running water and soak them in the water for 8 hours. Put in a pot the lentils with the water they have been soaking in.

Add a pinch of salt and cook for 1 hour or until they are tender. Turn off the heat and add the raw oil and the Parmesan.

● This is a single, good, nutritious dish.

★      ★      ★

## BOILED POTATOES AND COTECHINO SAUSAGE

*Ingredients for 2 servings:*

**10½ oz. potatoes**
**10½ oz. cotechino sausage**
   **salt**

Take the cotechino and poke the skin in a few places with a fork. Put it in a pot with 1 quart of water. Simmer for at least 1½ hours.

While the cotechino cooks, wash the potatoes and put them in a pot, cover with cold water, and boil for 20 minutes (20 minutes from when the water begins boiling).

Put the boiled cotechino on a cutting board, remove the skin, and slice. Add the boiled potatoes, which have been skinned and salted, to the sliced cotechino. Potatoes and cotechino "wed" well: the richness of the cotechino complements the plain potatoes.

● Together they make a complete dish, tasty and digestible. All that's needed is the usual fresh salad.

## GNOCCHI, ROMAN STYLE

*Ingredients for 2 servings:*

**7 oz. semolina**
**1 qt. milk**
   **salt**
**2 tablespoons butter**
**1 egg**
   **Parmesan cheese, to taste**

Put the milk in a pot, add 1 tablespoon of salt, and bring to a boil.

When it boils slowly add the semolina, stirring with a wooden spoon or a whisk. When the semolina has been added, continue cooking for 20 minutes, stirring occasionally. Turn off the heat and add the egg, mixing vigorously to blend smoothly.

Take a large serving platter or tray, wet the plate, and pour the mixture in the plate, smoothing it out till it's about ¾ inch high. Cool and cut into circles with a pasta cutter or a glass.

Grease a pan or baking dish. Spread the pasta circles out in the pan and dot with butter and a little Parmesan. Put in another layer of gnocchi and season them. Continue making layers until there are no more gnocchi. Top with butter and Parmesan.

Bake in a hot oven at 475° until the top is golden brown.

• This can be a single, nutritious, and wholesome dish. It's good to accompany it with a fresh fruit salad.

*Note:* The scraps of dough are put between layers filling in the empty spaces.

★     ★     ★

## ITALIAN DANDELION WITH SMOKED BACON

*Ingredients for 2 servings:*

**17½ oz. Italian dandelion
  4 tablespoons olive oil
  5 oz. smoked bacon
    salt**

Clean and wash the dandelion well.

Heat 2 cups of water in a pot with 1 teaspoon of salt. When the water boils add the dandelion (all green vegetables are cooked in boiling salted water: only in this way will they remain green—the amount of water must be small otherwise the nutrients will be uselessly lost) and boil for 20 minutes.

While the vegetable boils cut the bacon into pieces. Put the oil in a skillet, add the bacon, and brown it. Add the boiled dandelion, squeezed and finely chopped, to the bacon.

Mix and cook another 4 minutes.

● This is a wholesome dish. Dandelion is good for you. It's detoxifying and rich in iron and important minerals. The bacon's fat is easy to digest. The wonderful smell makes the stomach happily await its guest!

In this case, it is a wholesome dish, but it requires a piece of cheese to guarantee the presence of protein.

## CHEESE STEAKS

*Ingredients for 2 servings:*

**2 slices of provolone cheese about 5 oz. each**
**1 egg**
**2 tablespoons bread crumbs**
  **olive oil**

Buy 2 slices of mild provolone and remove the skin.

Put the egg in a plate, no salt because the cheese is salty. Beat the egg with a fork. Dip the cheese slices in the egg and then in the bread crumbs (like cutlets).

Put a glass of olive oil in an iron skillet and fry the cheese steaks like cutlets. They are excellent if eaten immediately.

● A worthy accompaniment is an abundant mixed salad. Enough!

★　　★　　★

## BAKED SARDINES AND POTATOES

*Ingredients for 2 servings:*

10½  oz. fresh sardines, cleaned
14  oz. potatoes
 6  tablespoons oil
 4  tablespoons Parmesan cheese
 1  pinch oregano
    salt

Buy fresh sardines (ask the fish vendor to clean them and remove the spine).

Wash and dry the sardines. Peel, wash, and thinly slice the potatoes. Take a baking pan, add a little oil, and spread a layer of potatoes in the oil.

Add a little salt, oregano, and Parmesan, and lay the sardines on top of the potatoes. Then add a little oil. More potatoes, salt, oregano, Parmesan, sardines, oil. Finish with potatoes, salt, oregano, Parmesan, and oil.

Bake in a hot oven at 475° for 45 minutes. If the top becomes too brown, cover with aluminum foil.

• They are excellent, all that's needed is the usual salad or a fruit salad.

★          ★          ★

## PORK ROAST WITH POTATOES

*Ingredients for 2 servings:*

14  oz. pork loin
10½  oz. potatoes
 2  tablespoons oil
 1  sprig rosemary
 1  small glass white wine

In a saucepan put the oil, the rosemary, and the meat.

Brown the meat on all sides. It's best to brown the meat over high heat so that the meat will quickly form a crust trapping all the important nutrients by sealing in the juices.

After browning the meat, add salt and the dry white wine. Let the wine evaporate, cover, and cook for 15 minutes. Meanwhile, peel the potatoes, wash and dry them, and cut them into pieces.

Add the potatoes to the pork and continue cooking together for 30 minutes more.

● Here is a very good and complete dish. As you see, the potatoes absorb the juice from the roast, and when you eat them you regain all the nutrients!

★　　　★　　　★

## ANCHOVIES WITH LEMON JUICE

*Ingredients for 2 servings:*

**10½ oz. fresh anchovies
    juice of 2 lemons
    salt
    pepper
    oregano
    olive oil**

Clean the anchovies carefully, removing the skin and spine (have the fish vendor do it), and put them in a baking dish.

Sprinkle with lemon juice (there must be plenty of juice: if 2 lemons are not enough add more). Cover with plastic wrap and refrigerate for 24 hours. After 12 hours turn them so that both sides marinate (the lemon juice serves to "cook" the anchovies, a little like "Meat, Alba Style").

When you're ready to serve them, transfer the anchovies to a serving platter. Season with a pinch of salt, oregano, pepper, and a little olive oil.

● These anchovies are very good and easy to digest. I suggest accompanying them with potatoes with green sauce, or a carrot salad.

Fish is rich in phosphorus and important protein.

Anchovies are one of the fish richest in the primary nutrients!

★　　　★　　　★

**Difficulties at the End of the Month**

Spaghetti with Oil and Rosemary
Pasta with Arugola
Polenta
Polenta with Pepper and Olive Oil
Stale Bread Pie
Gnocchi, Roman Style
Lentils with Oil and Cheese
Boiled Potatoes and Cotechino
Italian Dandelion with Smoked Bacon
Pork Roast with Potatoes
Steak with Cheese
Baked Sardines and Potatoes
Anchovies with Lemon Juice

# 10

## WHEN YOU MAKE MISTAKES (ADVANCED COOKING)

*It sometimes happens that you carefully read a recipe, try to understand it, do just as it says, and the result? A disaster! Don't worry. The majority of names of important dishes are the result of a recipe that failed originally but perhaps are better than the intended recipe. A failed dish can be a test for you: you can see if you're an optimistic and clever type; you should know how to laugh and baptize your "masterpieces."*

*Many times I've failed not within my home or community but during a lesson in front of many engaged couples. . . . Certainly it's not pleasant but it must be dealt with. If you don't want surprises be careful not to copy recipes from newspapers or books written by amateurs. In all modesty, I'd like to say that if you read my recipes it's doubtful you'll have to invent new titles. I have already done everything I can to spare you these insecure emotions.*

*If, however, something surprising does happen, write to me for I will gladly make note of it.*

*Be assured that if you make a mistake, there is always a remedy.*

# FROM MISTAKES TO ... MASTERPIECES

| | |
|---|---|
| Overcooked rice | Molds — croquettes — sweets stuffed vegetables — omelet |
| Potato Gnocchi which fall apart | Pie — omelet |
| Burned roast | Cut off the burned part and season the good part with a good wine sauce |
| Very tough steak | Put through a meat grinder and make a pie or meatballs or hamburgers |
| Mold is raw in center | Cut into slices, bread them and fry them |
| Antipasto mistakes | Sauces + potatoes white sauce |
| Salty peppers | Add raw potatoes and cook again |
| Very salty steamed or boiled vegetables | Add stale bread and potatoes |
| Wrong quantities | Legumes which overflow the pot |
| Wrong quantities | Semolina without end |
| Sweets not fully cooked | Cut into slices and toast in the oven |
| Crazy cream | Add toasted, ground almonds |

# 11

## WHEN THE SCOUTS GO CAMPING

*It is well known that the scouts know how to do everything. They know how to get together and evaluate the talents of one another. They are capable of cooking, playing, and living every moment in the most constructive way possible. Even at camp they are champions. Timidly, I can offer a modest contribution knowing that the scouts:*

a) *never spend too much money:*
   *therefore, the dishes must be economical;*
b) *have no full-time cooks, only children who pass the day in various ways:*
   *therefore, the recipes must be easy and fast;*
c) *don't have refrigerators and electric appliances at their disposal because they live in a tent:*
   *therefore, the recipes must be for nonperishable foods;*
d) *need to stay healthy:*
   *therefore, the recipes must concern natural foods, few canned goods or preserved foods (precooked);*
e) *can also learn to make use of local products, which cost less and are fresher:*
   *therefore, it is necessary to collaborate with the local residents;*
   *if the camp is in the mountains, I suggest mountain products;*
   *if the camp is at the seashore, I suggest sea food;*
f) *are young people who need to nourish themselves well because, besides maintenance, they still have to grow, and living out in the open air quickly burns up their reserves:*
   *therefore, it is best to suggest cooking nutritious foods;*
g) *need to estimate the quantity of food to buy:*
   *therefore, the number of participants at camp must be*

> *taken into account (for example: bread: 10½ oz.
> each; pasta: 3½ oz. each; rice: 3½ oz. each; pastina:
> 1½ oz. each; meat: 5 oz. each, but if the meat has
> bones, 7 oz. each; cheese: 3½ oz. each; eggs: 2 each;
> fruit: 14 oz. each; raw vegetable: 3½ oz. each;
> cooked vegetable: 5 to 7 oz. each);*

h) *have need of listing the total shopping for the camp:
therefore, one must add up the expected quantities of
foods, multiply by the cost of a single product and
divide by the number of participants.*

*Isn't all this easy?*

# MENU FOR 7 DAYS (Can Be Repeated)

| Breakfast | Lunch | Supper |
|---|---|---|
| tea, milk<br>bread and mar-<br>    malade | pasta with oil and garlic<br>Hunter's stew with<br>    potatoes<br>6 oz. bread, fruit | pastina in broth<br>tuna and peas<br>bread and fruit |
| tea, milk<br>bread with<br>chocolate spread | rice with peas<br>hamburger and mixed<br>    salad<br>bread, fruit | potatoes and rice in<br>    broth<br>Zucchini and onion<br>    omelet<br>bread, fruit |
| tea, milk<br>bread and honey | pasta with bacon,<br>cheese, and eggs<br>barbecued chicken<br>potato and olive salad<br>bread, fruit | rice and milk soup<br>poached eggs<br>tomato and basil salad<br>bread, fruit |
| tea, milk<br>bread with butter<br>and sugar | tomato risotto<br>rabbit with butter<br>    and sage<br>string bean salad<br>bread, fruit | cream of nettle soup<br>barbecued frankfurters<br>    and peppers<br>bread, fruit |
| tea, milk<br>bread with butter<br>and jelly | Sardinian gnocchi with<br>    cheese<br>barbecued salt cod<br>boiled zucchini with<br>    capers and mint<br>bread, fruit | tomato soup<br>beef scallopini with<br>    tomato and oregano<br>sunflower and salad<br>bread, fruit |
| tea, milk<br>bread and honey | minestrone soup<br>barbecued pork cutlets<br>cabbage salad<br>bread, fruit | cream of water cress<br>    soup<br>mackerel and boiled<br>    carrots<br>bread, fruit |
| tea, milk<br>bread and nutella<br>    (chocolate<br>    spread) | noodles with butter<br>    and nuts<br>meat and prune kabobs<br>bread, fruit | paradise soup<br>barbecued salami<br>potatoes cooked in<br>    ashes<br>bread, cooked fruit |

# First Courses

## PASTA WITH GARLIC, OIL, AND HOT PEPPER

*Ingredients for 6 servings:*

21 oz. pasta
 1 medium glass olive oil
 6 cloves garlic
 1 small, hot pepper
 2 tablespoons salt

Bring to a boil a pot with 2 quarts of water and salt.

When the water boils add the pasta and stir well to separate. Cook for the time indicated on the package. If it's not written on the package calculate about 8-10 minutes.

While the pasta is cooking peel the garlic and put it in a skillet with the oil, then add the pepper (if you like it spicier crumble the pepper or use a pinch of hot pepper flakes).

In the oil sauté the garlic and pepper, but slowly just until the garlic becomes golden, not burned. If you're cooking over coals it's always better to use an aluminum pan: it facilitates cooking faster. Drain the pasta and season with the prepared condiment.

Parmesan cheese is not used! It will be ready in 45 minutes. If cooking on a gas stove, obviously, you'll have it ready in 30 minutes.

★     ★     ★

## RICE WITH PEAS

*Ingredients for 6 servings:*

**21 oz. rice**
**4 tablespoons butter**
**6 tablespoons Parmesan cheese**
**2 tablespoons salt**
**9 oz. fresh shelled peas**
**1½ qts. water**

Bring the salted water to a boil. Add the rice and peas and bring to a boil again over high heat. Then lower the heat and simmer for 15 minutes, stirring frequently and adding some hot water if needed.

At this point the rice should be dry but not too dry. Remove from heat and add the butter and Parmesan. Mix until the butter melts. Use sweet, natural butter.

*Note:* After cooking, 2 tablespoons of chopped parsley or raw tomato sauce may be added.

## RICE WITH RAW TOMATO

*Ingredients for 6 servings:*

**21 oz. rice**
**17½ oz. plum tomatoes**
**3 sprigs basil**
**1 small bunch parsley**
**1 rib celery**
**1 glass olive oil**
**6 tablespoons Parmesan cheese**
**2 tablespoons salt**
**1½ qts. water**

Bring the salted water to a boil in a pot. Add the rice and cook for 15 minutes.

Stir occasionally and cook uncovered. While the rice is cooking wash the tomatoes, parsley, basil, and celery. Finely chop the vegetables on a cutting board. If you are fortunate enough to have a food processor you can do it more easily. Gather the juice into a bowl and add the oil and 2 pinches of salt. Mix.

When the rice is cooked, turn off the heat and season the rice with the Parmesan and the raw sauce. Mix and serve.

● This is a light risotto. The raw tomatoes and herbs retain their vitamims and all their nutrients.

★      ★      ★

## PASTA WITH BACON, CHEESE, AND EGGS

*Ingredients for 6 servings:*

21  oz. pasta
12  oz. smoked bacon
 6  eggs
 6  tablespoons Parmesan cheese
 2  tablespoons olive oil
    salt

Bring to a boil 2 quarts of salted water (a handful of salt).

When the water boils add the pasta and mix to separate. Boil for the length of time indicated on the package. While the pasta is cooking, remove the rind from the bacon (it can be used to flavor vegetable soup!), cut the bacon into cubes, and put it in a frying pan with 2 tablespoons of oil.

Brown the bacon till crispy. Put the eggs and cheese in a bowl and beat them together with a fork or whisk.

Drain the pasta well and pour it into the bowl with the eggs; mix quickly so that the heat of the pasta will cook the eggs. Mix well, add the crisp, hot bacon. Mix again and serve.

- It's excellent.

## MINESTRONE SOUP

*Ingredients for 6 servings:*

5 oz. beets
  or
5 oz. lettuce or escarole
1 small head cabbage
1 pinch rosemary
1 red, hot pepper tip
4 potatoes
2 onions
2 carrots
12 slices Tuscan bread
  some garlic cloves
1 glass olive oil
6 tablespoons Parmesan cheese
  salt

Clean and wash all the vegetables, dice the carrots and potatoes, and slice the rest of the vegetables.

Sauté the onions in a pan with ½ glass of oil until golden in color. Add the rest of the vegetables, cover with 1½ quarts of water and 2 tablespoons of salt.

Cook over low heat for 40 minutes. Start counting from when the water begins boiling. While the minestrone is cooking, toast the slices of bread on the grill.

Toast them well on both sides and sauté the bread slices with garlic. In each soup dish put 2 slices of bread and 1 teaspoon of olive oil over the bread.

When you're ready to serve, pour the minestrone over the bread and complete the dish with a tablespoon of Parmesan.

- It's great!

★      ★      ★

## SARDINIAN GNOCCHI WITH CHEESE

*Ingredients for 6 servings:*

**17½ oz. Sardinian gnocchi**
 **2 oz. gorgonzola cheese**
 **2 oz. toma cheese**
 **2 oz. fresh ricotta cheese**
 **2 oz. fontina cheese**
 **6 tablespoons Parmesan cheese**
 **4 tablespoons sweet, natural butter**
    **salt**

Heat a pot with 3 quarts of water (Sardinian gnocchi are made of durum wheat, very nutritious, and they need a lot of water to cook well). Add a handful of salt and bring to a boil.

When the water boils add the pasta, stir, and cook for at least 20 minutes.

While the pasta is cooking, dice all the cheese (remove the skin!). When the gnocchi are cooked, drain and return them to the pot in which they were cooked, add the assorted cheeses, the butter, and the Parmesan. Mix, and they're ready.

- They're good and nutritious.

★      ★      ★

## NOODLES WITH BUTTER, SAGE, AND NUTS

*Ingredients for 6 servings:*

**21 oz. noodles**
**2 oz. sweet, natural butter**
**2 sprigs sage**
**6 tablespoons Parmesan cheese**
**6 tablespoons chopped walnuts (7 oz. shelled walnuts)**

Heat a pot with 2 quarts of water and a handful of salt.

When the water boils, add the noodles, stir, and continue cooking. While the noodles are cooking, shell the nuts and chop them with a grinder or with scout ingenuity. In a small pan melt the butter and brown the sage.

Drain the noodles and season with the butter and sage, the Parmesan and nuts. Mix.

• It is a very tasty dish.

# Soups

### PASTINA IN BROTH

*Ingredients for 6 servings:*

7 dishes beef broth
10½ oz. pastina
6 tablespoons Parmesan cheese

Put the broth in a pot. Heat. When the broth boils add the pastina.

Cook for 7-10 minutes. Turn off the heat and add the Parmesan.

★     ★     ★

### POTATOES AND RICE IN BROTH

*Ingredients for 6 servings:*

3 large potatoes
9 oz. rice
6 teaspoons Parmesan cheese
2 tablespoons butter
  salt

Peel and wash the potatoes, then slice them.

In a pot put 7 soup dishes of cold water (take a soup dish and fill it with water as you would with soup and put 1 for each person + 1 extra into the pot). Add the potatoes and 1 tablespoon of salt. Bring to a boil, add the rice, and cook for 20 minutes. Turn off the heat and add the butter and Parmesan.

• It's nutritious, warm, and good for the stomach!

★     ★     ★

## RICE AND MILK SOUP

*Ingredients for 6 servings:*

10½ oz. rice
2 tablespoons butter
1½ qts. milk
½ teaspoon salt

Put the milk in a pot and add the rice and salt and half the butter. Cook over low heat stirring frequently (especially when it's almost cooked) so it doesn't stick to the bottom of the pan.

When it's cooked, turn off the heat, add the rest of the butter, and serve.

● This is a very nutritious dish.

★     ★     ★

## TOMATO SOUP

*Ingredients for 6 servings:*

2 lbs. ripe tomatoes
10½ oz. stale bread
3½ oz. virgin olive oil
4 cloves garlic
some sage and basil
1½ qts. beef broth
salt
pepper

Put the beef broth in a pot or an equal amount of water.

Add the tomatoes that have been ground or chopped; boil for 10 minutes. Slice the bread. Put the olive oil in a pot. Peel and crush the garlic and add it to the oil. Add the sage and basil, which have been washed and dried. Arrange the bread in the pot and brown on both sides.

When the bread is golden brown, add the tomatoes with the broth. Cook for 15 minutes, (If you use water instead of broth, remember to salt the water.)

● This is excellent soup—hot, warm, or cold.

★    ★    ★

**CREAM OF NETTLE SOUP**

*Ingredients for 6 servings:*

21 oz. young nettle leaves
 2 medium onions
 1 clove garlic
 1 pinch chopped mint
 3 heaping tablespoons corn starch (or 3 heaping tablespoons flour)
1½ qts. water
 6 tablespoons olive oil
   salt
   pepper

Put the oil in a saucepan and add the onions and the garlic, which have been washed and finely chopped.

If you use the flour, add it now and let it brown with the garlic and onion, add all the other ingredients (except the corn starch), and boil for 40-50 minutes. Blend the mixture in a blender. (If you don't have a blender, you must finely chop all the ingredients.)

At this point add the corn starch to the soup by first blending it with a couple of tablespoons of the soup. Return to boiling, stirring continuously to avoid lumps. As soon as the soup becomes creamy (after 3-4 minutes), it's ready to serve.

● This is an agreeable soup, good for delicate stomachs thanks to the nettles.

*Note:* There's a trick to gathering the nettles without pinching yourself: when you're about to pick them hold your breath! Try it and see! (At your own risk!)

★    ★    ★

## CREAM OF WATERCRESS SOUP

*Ingredients for 6 servings:*

**21 oz. wild watercress**
 **2 medium onions**
**½ glass oil**
 **2 teaspoons chopped parsley**
 **2 teaspoons chopped marjoram**
 **3 tablespoons potato starch**
**26 oz. milk**
**26 oz. water**
   **salt**
 **6 tablespoons Parmesan cheese**

Put the oil and finely chopped onion in a pot, then all the well-washed watercress (reserve a few tender leaves).

Add the marjoram and parsley and when the flavors are well blended add the milk and water. Cook uncovered for a half hour.

Blend the soup in the blender and return it to the pot, add the potato starch (previously dissolved in some water) stirring continuously to avoid lumps.

When the mixture becomes creamy, add the raw watercress leaves and dish up the soup, sprinkling with a tablespoon of Parmesan on each portion.

## PARADISE SOUP

*Ingredients for 6 servings:*

1½ qts. beef broth
5 eggs
6 tablespoons crushed bread
6 tablespoons Parmesan cheese
  nutmeg

Put the beef broth in a pot and bring to a boil.

Meanwhile prepare the doughy mixture like this: put the eggs in a bowl and beat well with a fork, then add the bread, Parmesan, and a little nutmeg. Mix together well.

When the broth boils, pour in the doughy mixture all at once, cover, and bring the soup to a full boil without touching the dough. Boil for 2 minutes, mix, and serve.

• This is an excellent soup; it's light and quickly digested as well as being very nutritious.

★          ★          ★

# Meat and Vegetables for Lunch

## HUNTER'S STYLE STEW WITH POTATOES

*Ingredients for 6 servings:*

21 oz. beef for stew
 2 medium onions
 1 sprig sage
 1 sprig rosemary
 1 rib celery
 1 glass white wine
17½ oz. fresh or peeled tomatoes
28 oz. potatoes
 1 glass oil
 2 teaspoons salt

Clean and wash the herbs, celery, and onions.

Use a pot large enough to hold the meat and potatoes. In the pot put the oil, the chopped herbs, chopped celery and onions, and the meat. Brown over high heat. When the meat is well browned, add the salt and the wine.

Cover and cook for 20 minutes. While the meat cooks peel and wash the potatoes. Cut the potatoes into large cubes. After the meat has cooked for 20 minutes add the potatoes and let them absorb the flavors well.

Finally, add the fresh or peeled tomatoes that have been cut into pieces. Continue cooking for another 30 minutes.

- This is a good dish, healthy and economical.

## RABBIT WITH BUTTER AND SAGE, STRING BEAN SALAD

*Ingredients for 6 servings:*

**3 lbs. rabbit**
**2 oz. butter**
**3 sprigs sage**
**21 oz. fresh string beans**
  **salt**
  **oil**
  **vinegar**

Wash the rabbit and cut it into pieces. Calculate 2 pieces per person.

Heat a large skillet. Add the butter, sage, and rabbit to the skillet. Brown the rabbit over high heat, add salt, and cover. Lower the heat. Continue cooking over low heat for 45 minutes.

While the rabbit is cooking, heat a pot with a quart of water and a handful of salt to boiling. Meanwhile, clean and wash the beans. When the water boils, add the beans and boil for 30 minutes. Drain and then season them with oil and vinegar.

● This is a good dinner and it can be prepared in 45 minutes.

★          ★          ★

## BARBECUED CHICKEN, POTATO AND OLIVE SALAD

*Ingredients for 6 servings:*

> **3 lbs. chicken (it's better to buy 2 small chickens, about 1½ - 2 lbs. each; they'll cook better and it's easier to cut into portions)**
> **2 lemons**
> **8 tablespoons oil**
> **salt**
> **pepper**
> **28 oz. potatoes**
> **10½ oz. olives**
> **1 glass olive oil**
> **3 tablespoons wine vinegar**
> **2 teaspoons salt**

Wash the potatoes without peeling them and put them in a pot with cold water. Cook for 20 minutes.

While the potatoes boil, clean the chicken, cut it in half, and dispose of the insides. Pound the 2 halves to flatten them a little. Brush the 4 halves of chicken with oil. Add salt and pepper (calculate ½ teaspoon of salt and a pinch of pepper for each half of chicken).

Heat the grill well, set the chicken on the grill, and cook over high heat: the meat should be well cooked and the outside very crispy. Serve with lemon slices.

While the chicken is cooking, peel the boiled potatoes, slice them in a bowl, add the olives, and season with oil, salt, and vinegar.

★          ★          ★

## BARBECUED COD AND BOILED ZUCCHINI WITH CAPERS AND MINT

*Ingredients for 6 servings:*

2½ lbs. salt cod
3 lemons
2 sprigs rosemary
  oil
  salt
  pepper
2 lbs. fresh zucchini
1 tablespoon capers
1 pinch mint
  oil
  salt
  vinegar

Cut the cod into pieces, wash, and dry it well.

Prepare the marinating mixture with a glass of oil, lemon juice, 3 pinches of salt, and a pinch of pepper. Put the cod in a bowl.

Pour the marinating mixture over the cod and let it marinate about an hour, turning the pieces of fish occasionally. Take a sheet of aluminum foil, brush it well with oil, and put it on the hot grill. Arrange the pieces of codfish on the foil and sprinkle with the marinade and the rosemary leaves. Cook the fish for 20 minutes, turning occasionally with a spatula,

While the fish is cooking, heat a pot with 1 quart of water and a handful of salt. When the water boils, add the cleaned zucchini (cut off the stem) and wash them. Boil for 20 minutes. Remove the zucchini from the water (the water can be used for soup; it's good to save the water from green vegetables: it has important nutrients) and as soon as possible slice them into circles.

Season the zucchini with vinegar, oil, minced mint leaves, and capers. Mix.

• They are tasty!

## HAMBURGER AND MIXED SALAD

*Ingredients for 6 servings:*

6 hamburgers, about 3½ oz. each
1 sprig rosemary
  salt
  pepper
21 oz. mixed salad
  *To season:*
1 glass olive oil
3 pinches salt
3 tablespoons wine vinegar

Put a sheet of aluminum foil on the grill and heat the grill and the foil.

When it's hot, put the meat on the foil. Brown on one side (5 minutes). Turn the meat and add salt. Sprinkle some rosemary leaves on each hamburger. Continue cooking 5 minutes more. The aluminum foil prevents the meat juices from dripping on the coals wasting the nutrients.

Clean the salad greens and wash well. It is pleasant and intelligent to use 2 or 3 types of salad greens, for example, lettuce, arugola, endive, red radishes, tomatoes, peppers, onions. Look for local greens. Drain the salad and season with salt, vinegar, and oil. Mix and serve.

• It's very good for you!

★    ★    ★

## BARBECUED PORK CHOPS, CABBAGE SALAD

*Ingredients for 6 servings:*

- 6 **pork chops, about 5 oz. each**
  **oil**
  **salt**
  **pepper**
- 3 **sprigs rosemary**
- 21 **oz. Savoy cabbage (it's easier to digest)**
- 1 **glass vinegar**

On each pork chop put a little salt, pepper, and oil.

Put a sheet of aluminum foil on the hot grill. Arrange the chops. Put the rosemary on the chops and brown well on both sides. In the meantime, clean the cabbage (remove the stalk and any unsightly leaves that can be used in minestrone as long as they are not yellow or decayed) and wash it.

Taking a cutting board and a good sharp knife cut the cabbage in half and patiently slice it thinly in the best way possible. Put it in a salad bowl and season with salt, vinegar, and oil. Mix well. Season the salad at least 1 hour before serving.

- This is certainly a dish for strong people!

★     ★     ★

## MEAT KABOBS WITH PRUNES, FRIED POTATOES

*Ingredients for 6 servings:*

1½ lbs. lean beef
30 prunes, approximately
1 good pinch thyme
  laurel leaves
  oil
  salt
  pepper
2 lbs. potatoes
1 qt. frying oil (to be reused)
  salt

Put the prunes in a bowl and cover them with warm water to soften them.

Cut the meat into good-sized chunks. Thread the meat onto skewers alternating the prunes with the chunks of meat and some laurel leaves. Sprinkle the kabobs with salt, pepper, and thyme, brush with oil, and cook on a very hot grill, turning often and brushing them with oil occasionally.

Serve them hot and golden.

While the kabobs are cooking, heat a pot with 1 quart of olive oil. When the oil boils add the peeled potatoes, which have been washed and sliced as you like. Cook to a golden color, remove them from the oil, and add salt.

• Today is really a feast!

# Main Courses and Vegetables for Supper

## TUNA AND PEAS

*Ingredients for 6 servings:*

2 oz. tuna per person (it's worthwhile to buy a large
fish, for example, about 6½ lbs. You get more out
of it and it's more solid. The small cans are full of
discarded and small bits of tuna and you don't
get much out of them!)
4 oz. fresh peas per person, 3 oz. if canned
2 oz. butter
1 sprig sage
some lettuce leaves
salt

Put the butter and sage in a pan, add the fresh or
canned peas (if you use the canned, it's best to take them
out of the can, put them in a colander, and rinse them
under running water).

Cook the fresh peas for 20 minutes, canned peas for 5
minutes. Add salt.

Wash and dry the lettuce leaves well. On each leaf
put 2 oz. of tuna and serve with peas on the side.

• Peas with tuna is an excellent, nutritious dish.

★     ★     ★

## ONION AND ZUCCHINI OMELET

*Ingredients for 6 servings:*

   6  eggs
10½  oz. onions
10½  oz. zucchini
   2  tablespoons olive oil
   1  glass milk
      nutmeg
   6  pinches salt
   6  tablespoons Parmesan cheese

Clean the onions and zucchini, then wash and dry them.

In a large skillet put 4 tablespoons of butter and add the thinly sliced onions and zucchini. Cover and cook for 15 minutes over moderate heat. Add salt.

While the vegetable is cooking, combine the eggs, salt, Parmesan, a sprinkle of nutmeg, and the milk in a bowl. Beat well with a fork to blend. When the vegetable is cooked, add the egg mixture, cover the skillet, and cook for 3-5 minutes. With the help of the cover, turn the omelet. Continue cooking 5 minutes more. It's ready.

## FRANKFURTERS AND ROASTED PEPPERS

*Ingredients for 6 servings:*

12  medium frankfurters
 6  yellow or red, meaty peppers
 2  cloves garlic
    a handful of parsley
 6  tablespoons oil
 6  pinches salt
 1  pinch pepper

Wash and dry the peppers well and roast them on the hot grill, turning them occasionally. Leave them on the grill until they are well-shriveled.

Let them cool, peel them, cut them open, discard the seeds, and cut them into pieces. Prepare a little sauce with oil, garlic, chopped parsley, salt, and pepper.

Pour this over the peppers and set aside for a few minutes before serving. Then, while the grill is very hot, barbecue the frankfurters, browning them well on both sides: they should be very hot and browned.

They're ready.

★　　★　　★

## BEEF SCALLOPINI WITH TOMATO AND OREGANO, SUNFLOWER SALAD

*Ingredients for 6 servings:*

  6  beef cutlets, about 3 oz. each
  6  slices mozzarella cheese
     or
  6  slices American cheese
10½  oz. fresh or canned, peeled tomatoes
  1  pinch oregano
  1  glass olive oil
  3  tablespoons flour
17½  oz. mountain sunflowers
     or
17½  oz. fresh salad
  6  tablespoons olive oil
  2  pinches salt
  2  tablespoons vinegar

In a large skillet put a glass of oil, then heat. Coat the beef with flour and add the meat to the skillet.

Brown the meat on both sides and add salt. On each slice of meat put a slice of cheese, a piece of tomato, and a pinch of oregano. Cover the skillet and cook over low heat for 15 minutes.

While the meat is cooking clean the salad, wash and dry it well, and season with salt, vinegar, and oil. Mix well.

• Remember that sunflowers are very rich in vitamins and minerals.

★     ★     ★

## MACKEREL AND BOILED CARROTS WITH PARSLEY AND MUSTARD

*Ingredients for 6 servings:*

21 oz. canned mackerel
21 oz. carrots
    a handful of parsley
 1 tablespoon mustard
 2 tablespoons vinegar
 6 tablespoons olive oil
 3 pinches salt
 1 tablespoon salt

Scrape the carrots and put them in a pot with 1 quart of cold water and 1 tablespoon of salt. Bring to a boil.

Cook for 30 minutes. Remove the carrots from the water (don't throw the water away, it can be used for soup or vegetable broth!) and as soon as they are cool slice them in a bowl. Season the carrots with salt, vinegar, oil, chopped parsley, and mustard. Mix well.

Put the mackerel, divided into 6 portions, on a plate and add the carrot salad.

• The mackerel is nutritious because of the proteins and minerals it contains. The carrots, prepared in this way, guarantee vitamins.

★     ★     ★

### POACHED EGGS WITH TOMATO AND BASIL SALAD

*Ingredients for 6 servings:*

6 fresh eggs
1 qt. water
1 tablespoon vinegar
1 tablespoon salt
6 anchovy fillets in oil
2 lbs. tomatoes
1 sprig basil
6 tablespoons olive oil
1 tablespoon vinegar
6 pinches salt

In a pot put a quart of water with 1 tablespoon of salt and 1 tablespoon of vinegar.

Bring to a boil. When the water boils break the eggs (if they don't fit all together, cook 3 at a time). Boil for 3 minutes or, better yet, just until the white of the egg solidifies making the yolk disappear. With a slotted spoon remove the poached eggs and put them in a serving platter.

Decorate the eggs with the anchovies: they're ready!

● They are very digestible and nutritious because the white is well cooked but not the yolk: in fact, the yolk is more digestible raw.

Wash the tomatoes, slice them, and season with salt, vinegar, oil, and the washed, chopped basil.

Tomatoes are rich in vitamins and minerals.

★      ★      ★

## BARBECUED SAUSAGES, POTATOES COOKED IN ASHES

*Ingredients for 6 servings:*

**12 "salamini" — boar's meat sausages**
**12 potatoes**
    **salt**
    **oil**
    **aluminum foil**

First, cook the potatoes. Wrap them 2 by 2 in aluminum foil and put them under the ashes. They'll cook in about 45 minutes. While the potatoes are cooking put the sausages on the grill pricking them so the fat will run out. Brown them well on all sides: they're ready.

• Remember that everything cooked on a barbecue is healthier and more tasty.

Remove the potatoes from the ashes, peel and slice them, and season with oil and salt. They are excellent even without seasoning if you accompany them with the sausages that are already tasty and spicy.

# 12

# WHEN THE FAMILY IS EXPECTING A BABY

*When we talk of diet, we think of some terrible thing, of some illness, or of sacrifices! This is a mistake because there exists a diet that allows for a rational growth and there exist special diets for special cases.*

*Pregnancy is not an illness but an important occasion to finally follow a healthy diet.*

*The mother's duty is to offer her baby "in the making" the best that exists in nature. It's a little like having a guest to whom you offer the best things.*

*It is also a good occasion to begin to give the baby a good example, eating things that are good for you with the same joy as eating things that you like. The baby knows and is aware of everything.*

*To facilitate this program I suggest that during the pregnancy both mother and father eat the same food. In this way they help each other and the child already present in their lives.*

## Nutritive Needs of the Baby

Everyone believes that pregnancy calls for a high consumption of nutritious foods, since along with the needs of the mother, the needs of the baby also must be satisfied. This opinion, only partially justifiable, can be summarized in the popular saying that a "pregnant woman must eat for two."

This misleading opinion first goes counter to the actual necessities of the two bodies and second can cause numerous problems.

Naturally, nourishment is your major demand but there is a notable difference between "substantial nourishment" and "hypernutrition." However, it is true that the baby is nourished with the substances in the foods that the mother eats. If these are not consumed in sufficient quantities, disturbances or real pathological problems can occur in the mother as well as the child.

The right approach consists in a diet that is slightly superior to the normal quantity-wise and above all well balanced quality-wise. To achieve this a very varied diet is needed to prevent the future mother, considering the particular hormonal situation at the moment, from gaining too much weight, or worse, experiencing serious metabolical disturbances like toxemia.

In order for it to be balanced, a pregnant woman's diet not only must contain all that she needs but also must be in the right proportions. Above all, a sufficient amount of proteins are needed, proteins that will work together in the formation of a new being. Two thirds or at least half of these must be animal proteins because they are "complete," that is, they contain all the essential amino acids.

Among the animal proteins it is best to choose, besides meat that can cause conditions or incompatibilities, fish, eggs, and milk and dairy products, particularly precious because they supply the mother with calcium, which is indispensable in the formation of the new skeleton. It is also essential to guarantee, through diet, an abundant supply of iron, not only not to impoverish the mother's reserves but also to supply the baby with a sufficient amount of a substance that he or she will be deprived of during the whole time he or she is on milk. In fact, iron is one of the very few important nutrients that milk lacks. Foods rich in iron are: liver, cocoa, eggs, spinach, parsley, and a fruit not well known or widespread, the blueberry.

Fats and carbohydrates must be present in the diet, in the minimum quantities necessary so as to avoid too much weight gain, which always ends up being harmful. Among the fats, a discreet amount of animal fats must be eaten to guarantee a sufficient contribution of liposoluble vitamins, but always raw so as not to overwork the digestive system and to prevent acidity. *Plenty of fruit and vegetables must be taken but little salt.* Fruit and vegetables, eaten in abundance and variety, facilitate intestinal functions that have normally slowed up and at the same time provide all the necessary vitamins and minerals. In the last months Vitamin K can be particularly important for its anti-hemorrhaging quality needed at the moment of delivery. This vitamin is found in considerable quantity in tomatoes and spinach. Intake of sodium chloride, common table salt, must be minimal not only to limit the retention of water and the consequential appearance of edema but also to shorten labor and make it less painful.

## Diet for a Pregnant Woman — General Rules

### Breakfast:

Milk, or coffee, or tea, or yogurt, or cappuccino, or fruit, all sweetened with honey if possible, plus 3-4 slices of toast with marmalade without artificial colors.

For the first few months, if you work, you can eat a roll with prosciutto or fresh cheese, keeping in mind that you shouldn't eat more than 3½ oz. of bread or 3 oz. of breadsticks or 3 oz. of pasta per day.

### 10:00 A.M.:

1 glass of milk or yogurt or a fruit (apple).

### 1:00 P.M.:

Instead of a first course, a dish of raw vegetables (carrots, salad, cabbage, etc.).

Second course rich in proteins and minerals. Meat or fish or prosciutto or fresh (not aged) cheese, or eggs. The meat and fish (at least 5 oz.) should be cooked (steamed, boiled, broiled, or baked), and so should the eggs (at least 2).

Plenty of cooked vegetables.

2 oz. of bread, if not already eaten at 8 A.M. or 10 A.M.

Fruit, 1 cup of coffee, 1 glass of wine if you want it.

**5:00 P.M.:**

Tea, or milk, or yogurt, or fruit.

**6:00 P.M.:**

*First course:* minestrone or boiled vegetable with raw oil and Parmesan cheese. Once a week you can add pasta and twice a week rice. Or you can substitute risotto or pasta for the minestrone or the boiled vegetable.

Meat broth increases stomach acidity because it increases the production of acids.

*Second course:* the same as at lunch alternating meat with fish, etc. Then cooked or raw vegetables and fruit.

All the food must have little seasoning and little salt.

Taking into account the liquids ingested, you shouldn't have less than 1-1½ quarts per day of water, fruit, and other liquids; the water should be natural, not carbonated.

Exclude from the diet: fats, fried foods, sweets of every kind, sauces, sausages, ice cream, liquor, and more than 2 cups of coffee a day, smoking, drugs, raw meat.

Moderate: amounts of starches, legumes, fruit (very sweet) containing a lot of sugar (grapes, figs), dried fruit.

Increase: foods containing iron, calcium, and vitamins.

Once or twice a week: 1 serving of caramel cream, or 1 serving of homemade ice cream.

A pregnant woman's diet must be balanced with the right proportions of proteins, vitamins, and minerals because her body is creating a new person, an individual who will have a skeleton and organs ready to function from the moment of birth.

A pregnant woman must nourish herself in a way that will not put too much stress on her liver or kidneys, which are the organs appointed to filter the wastes from her own body and those of the baby.

## CREAMED VEGETABLES

| Amount: | Seasoning: | Alternative Seasoning: |
|---------|------------|------------------------|
| 7 oz. | Extra-virgin<br>olive oil | Raw tomato<br>Special pesto<br>Chopped herbs |

### Classic Creamed Vegetables

7 oz. of potatoes, onions, carrots, celery, peas, string beans, tomatoes, zucchini, basil, a little salt, and 1 quart of water. Cook 1-3 hours. After cooking add olive oil, if you like, Parmesan cheese or the alternate seasonings proposed.

### Creamed Vegetables and Sunflowers

Classic creamed vegetables plus 10½ oz. of sunflowers. Among vegetables, sunflowers are the richest in vitamins and minerals.

### Creamed Vegetables and Nettles

7 oz. of potatoes, carrots, onions, and peas, 14 oz. of fresh nettle tops, a little salt, and 1 quart of water. Cook about 2 hours.

Nettles contain: iron, magnesium, sodium, potassium, calcium, sulphur, manganese, and other minerals, Vitamin A and Vitamin B1.

### Creamed Vegetables with Fennel

Classic creamed vegetables plus 14 oz. of fennel (better if it's wild fennel: then all you need is 7 oz.).

### Creamed Zucchini and Basil

14 oz. of fresh zucchini, a handful of basil, 1 quart of water, and a little salt. Cook 30 minutes.

### Creamed Spinach

7 oz. of potatoes, onions, carrots, lettuce, and basil, 10½ oz. of spinach, 1 quart of water, and a little salt. Cook 1½ hours.

### Creamed Watercress

7 oz. of potatoes, onions, carrots, watercress, parsley, and basil, a little salt, and 1 quart of water. Cook 1½ hours.

*Note:* As you see, a dominant seasonal vegetable is all you need to have a creamed vegetable dish with flavor and a different nutritive value.

## PASTA AND RICE

| Allowance: | Condiment: | Alternative Condiments: |
|---|---|---|
| 3½ oz. | Extra-virgin olive oil | Raw tomato and basil |
| | Parmesan cheese | Oil and basil |
| | | Ricotta cheese and oil |
| | | Special pesto |
| | | Tomato and mozzarella |
| | | Cheeses |

### Noodles, Raw Tomato, and Basil

3½ oz. fresh or peeled tomatoes and 10 leaves of basil, chopped.

### Spaghetti with Oil and Basil

2 tablespoons of oil and 10 leaves of basil, chopped.

### Macaroni with Ricotta and Oil

3½ oz. of ricotta and 2 tablespoons of oil.

### Gnocchi with Special Pesto

2 tablespoons of pesto sauce.

### Fusilli Macaroni with Tomato and Mozzarella

3½ oz. of tomato and ½ mozzarella, chopped.

### Bucatini Spaghetti with Fresh Cheese

3½ oz. of assorted cheeses, 2 tablespoons of Parmesan cheese.

### Green Gnocchi

See Index.

### Artichoke Risotto

See Index.

### Cheese Risotto

See Index.

### Pesto Risotto

See Gnocchi with Special Pesto.

### Green Risotto

Season with 7 oz. of herbs, steamed and put through a blender, add 1 tablespoon of oil and 2 tablespoons of Parmesan cheese.

*Note:* It's best to cook the rice in water that is only lightly salted. For 3 oz. of rice you need 7 oz. of water and a pinch of salt.

## RAW VEGETABLES

Seasoned with oil, lemon, and herbs.

| Daily Allowance: | Basic Condiment: | Alternative Seasoning: |
|---|---|---|
| 7–10½ oz. | Extra-virgin olive oil | Oil, salt, pepper |
| | Lemon, salt | Oil, salt, chopped herbs |

### Artichoke Salad

Seasoned with salt, oil, lemon, and a few slices of Parmesan cheese. (It is rich in iron.)

### Carrot Salad

Seasoned with oil, lemon, salt, and parsley.

### Cardoons

Seasoned with oil, salt, and pepper.

### Raw Cabbage Salad

Shredded and seasoned with salt, vinegar, and oil. It is rich in vitamins and minerals.

### Gherkin Salad

Seasoned—after salting them and draining them of the juice that makes them indigestible—with oil and lemon.

### Fennel

Seasoned with oil, salt, and pepper.

### Raw Mushroom Salad

Not too often and not more than 4 oz., seasoned with lemon and oil.

### Salads

It's always advisable to use salad greens like sunflower, chicory, lambs lettuce, arugola, lettuce, wild chicory, and red chicory. They are the richest in vitamins. The white ones are more tender but poor in vitamins and minerals like Belgian lettuce, endive, and escarole.

Salad is excellent seasoned with salt, oil, and lemon or vinegar.

### Sweet Pepper Salad

Peppers are the vegetable richest in vitamin C.

### Tomato Salad with Basil

### Tomato, Mozzarella, and Oregano Salad

### Turnip Salad

### Celery Salad

★        ★        ★

# BOILED VEGETABLES AND SPECIAL PESTO

| Daily Allowance: | Basic Condiment: | Other Condiments: |
|---|---|---|
| 14–17½ oz. | Oil and lemon | Oil, lemon, chopped herbs<br>Parmesan cheese and tomatoes |

## Baked Eggplant with Tomato and Parmesan

Slice, salt, and stack the eggplants under a weighted can to eliminate water, then put them in a baking pan with raw tomato sauce, basil, plenty of Parmesan and mozzarella.

## Boiled Artichokes

Seasoned with oil, lemon, and salt.

## Boiled Asparagus

Seasoned with oil and lemon.

## Boiled Beets

Seasoned with oil and basil leaves.

## Boiled Brussel Sprouts

Seasoned with oil and Parmesan.

## Boiled Carrots

Seasoned with chopped parsley, oil, lemon, and salt.

## Boiled Catalonia (Italian Dandelion)

Seasoned with oil, lemon, and salt.

## Boiled Cauliflower

Grated with raw tomato sauce and Parmesan cheese.

## Boiled Cauliflower

Seasoned with oil, lemon, and black olives.

## Boiled Fennel

Baked with Parmesan cheese.

**Boiled Onions**

Seasoned with special pesto.

**Boiled String Beans**

Seasoned with capers, oil, and mint.

**Boiled Turnip Tops**

Seasoned with oil and lemon.

**Boiled Zucchini**

Seasoned with oil, lemon, and chopped parsley.

**Broiled Porcini Mushrooms**

Then seasoned with oil and chopped parsley.

**Roasted Peppers**

Seasoned with oil.

**Steamed Spinach**

Seasoned with oil and Parmesan cheese.

**Special Pesto for Two**

16 leaves of basil, 2 tablespoons of Parmesan cheese, 2 tablespoons of toasted pine nuts (pignoli), 1 teaspoon of salt, 1 glass of extra-virgin olive oil.

Combine all the ingredients in a blender, blend 1 minute. It's ready.

● It's light, tasty and no contraindications for pregnant women, made like this!

★     ★     ★

**MEAT**

| Daily Allowance: | Condiment: | Alternative Seasoning: |
| --- | --- | --- |
| 5 oz. (cooked) | Oil and lemon | Rosemary<br>Sage |

**Beef Fillet**

Broiled or in foil.

**Rabbit Fillet**

Broiled or in foil.

**Turkey Fillet**

Broiled or in foil.

**Chicken Fillet**

Broiled or in foil.

**Hamburger**

Broiled.

**Hamburger**

Steamed.

**Hamburger**

Baked with mozzarella.

**Boiled Beef or Chicken or Rabbit**

In a salad.

**Beef Liver**

Broiled.

**Brains**

Baked.

**Guinea Hen**

In foil.

**Roast Beef**

In foil.

**Meat, Alba Style**

With horsemeat, or horsemeat alone.

**Raw Horsemeat**

And only horsemeat to avoid tapeworm and toxo-plasmosis.

### Broiled or Grilled Kabobs or Cooked in Foil

Made, however, only with rabbit, chicken, and beef. Alternate each piece with a sage leaf, salt, and wrap in aluminum foil. Bake in the oven at 475° for 30 minutes.

*Meat in Foil:* Take a sheet of aluminum foil, lay the selected meat on the foil, and flavor it with a little salt and aromatic herbs like rosemary, sage, and oregano.

Delicately wrap the meat in the foil, being careful not to tear the foil, otherwise the magic is ended! Bake in the oven at 475°. Calculate 1 hour for every 2 lbs. of meat.

• This is a very healthy way to cook. All the nutrients remain in the foil. No condiment is needed, nor much attention: it cooks by itself without having to be turned.

*Boiled Meats:* To have good boiled meat put the chosen meat in a pot with a little boiling water flavored with celery, onion, rosemary, basil, and salt. Cooking time varies with the type of meat and its weight. It's best to boil over low heat. A pressure cooker is excellent!

### FISH

| Daily Allowance: | Basic Seasoning: | Alternate Seasonings: |
| --- | --- | --- |
| 10½ - 14 oz. | Extra-virgin olive oil | Various herbs |

**Anchovies,** broiled or grilled.

**Whiting,** in foil.

**Porgy,** baked.

**Swordfish,** broiled.

**Sole,** steamed.

**Trout,** boiled.

**Shrimp,** in a salad.

**Sardines,** grilled.

**Octopus,** in a salad.

**Sand Shark,** baked.

For all these recipes see Index.

*Boiled Octopus:* if you want your boiled octopus to always be tender and good do this: heat a pot with 1 quart of water (good for an octopus from 21 oz. to 3 lbs.).

When the water boils put in the octopus (cleaned and washed) and boil for 45 minutes. After 45 minutes put a handful of salt in the pot. Boil 15 minutes more.

Turn off the heat and leave the octopus in the cooking water until it becomes cold.

Remove from the water and cut into pieces, season with oil, lemon, and parsley.

● It's very good, very nutritious and rich in phosphorus and other minerals and proteins.

## EGGS

*Daily Allowance: 2*

**"Prairie Oyster"**
**Soft-boiled Egg**
**Poached Egg on Toast**
**Eggs with Tuna and Mushrooms**
**Hard-boiled Egg**
**Hard-boiled Egg with Salt, Vinegar, and Oil.**

## Sample Menus:

| | BREAKFAST | 10 A.M. | 1 P.M. | 5 P.M. | SUPPER |
|---|---|---|---|---|---|
| M O N | Milk, toast, and honey | yogurt | broiled meat<br>raw or boiled vegetable<br>1 oz. bread<br>water, wine<br>fresh fruit, coffee | yogurt | creamed vegetable<br>fresh cheese<br>raw or boiled vegetable<br>1 oz. bread<br>fruit |
| T U E S | tea, Parmesan, bread sticks, 1 oz. | apple<br>glass of milk | risotto<br>boiled meat<br>raw or boiled vegetable<br>wine, fruit, coffee | apple<br>glass of milk | broiled fish<br>raw or boiled vegetable<br>1 oz. bread sticks<br>fruit, coffee |
| W E D | cappuccino<br>toast,<br>homemade<br>marmalade | homemade fruit<br>whip | octopus salad<br>raw or boiled vegetables<br>wine, bread<br>fruit, coffee | homemade fruit<br>whip | creamed vegetable<br>broiled liver<br>raw or cooked vegetable<br>fresh fruit |
| T H U R | yogurt, toast<br>honey | glass of milk<br>apple | pasta<br>broiled brains<br>raw or boiled vegetables<br>wine, fruit, coffee | glass of milk<br>apple | cooked or raw vegetable<br>prosciutto (cooked)<br>cheese<br>caramel cream |
| F R I | milk, toast<br>prosciutto (cooked) | apple | shrimp salad<br>cooked or raw vegetables<br>fruit sherbert<br>bread, coffee | apple | risotto<br>cooked or raw vegetables<br>fish in foil<br>fresh fruit |
| S A T | tea,<br>whole wheat toast<br>and mozzarella | glass of milk | broiled hamburger<br>cooked or raw vegetable<br>bread sticks, 1 oz.<br>wine, fruit, coffee | glass of milk | creamed vegetable<br>raw vegetable<br>fresh cheese kabobs<br>fruit salad |
| S U N | cappuccino<br>toast<br>marmalade | fruit whip | meat kabobs in foil<br>boiled vegetable with<br>special pesto<br>bread sticks<br>wine, ice cream | fruit whip | vegetable soup with rice<br>poached egg<br>raw vegetable<br>fresh fruit kabobs |

166

# PART TWO

1. **ANTIPASTO**
2. **SOUP**
3. **PASTA**
4. **RICE**
5. **MEAT**
6. **FISH**
7. **VEGETABLES**
8. **DESSERTS**
9. **SAUCES**
10. **HOMEMADE LIQUEURS, BEVERAGES, AND SHER-
    BERTS**
11. **HOMEMADE PRESERVES**

# 1

## ANTIPASTO

*Fantastic Mouthfuls — Chopped Veal, Viennese Style — Rice Salad — Six-Flavor Salad — Frankfurter Salad — Prosciutto Medallions in Gelatin — Pastry Dough — Tuna Pâté — Sandwiches — Stolen Sandwiches — Crepe Torte — Eggs with Tuna and Mushrooms — Poached Eggs in Aurora Sauce*

### FANTASTIC MOUTHFULS

*Ingredients for 6 servings:*

3½ oz. berna cheese, thickly sliced
3½ oz. fontina cheese
    pickled vegetables
    salami
    prosciutto
    frankfurters
    parsley
    radishes
    nuts
1 hard-boiled egg, crumbled
    wooden toothpicks

Cut the cheese into cubes. Over each cube put a little parsley, salami, and nuts; or frankfurters, prosciutto, pickled vegetables, and eggs; hold in place with a toothpick.

You'll make many tasty mouthfuls suitable for a cold supper or antipasto. You can, if you like, serve them on an apple or on a cabbage: that's very original!

★      ★      ★

## CHOPPED VEAL, VIENNESE STYLE

*Ingredients for 6 servings:*

3½ oz. chopped veal
2 oz. pickled mushrooms
2 oz. tuna
  one yolk mayonnaise
5 or 6 pastry tarts

Put the chopped meat in a narrow container.

Cover it with 1 glass of white vinegar, add some garlic cloves, and let it marinate for at least 6 hours. Take the meat out of the vinegar and drain. Chop the mushrooms and the tuna. Add them to the meat. Season with mayonnaise and mix.

● This is an excellent antipasto that can be served in pastry tarts or dough baskets or in lettuce leaves or even in tomatoes. Decorate with additional mayonnaise and parsley.

★        ★        ★

## RICE SALAD

*Ingredients for 2 servings:*

2 oz. rice
  frankfurters
  hard-boiled eggs
  sliced carrots, fennel, radishes
  pickled vegetables
  olives
  prosciutto
  Spanish string beans, peas, tomatoes, onions
  roasted or raw peppers
  artichokes
  walnuts
  berna cheese, fontina cheese, salami
  oil
  lemon
  etc.

Cook the rice for 12 minutes in boiling, salted water, drain, and rinse under cold water to stop the cooking process and remove the starch. Let it drain. In the meantime, chop all the ingredients (except the beans and the peas).

Combine everything in a glass bowl. Add the rice and season with salt, pepper, and lemon. Mix well.

● The resulting dish is cheery, appetizing, and nutritious.

It's excellent for a cold supper at the beach or on a picnic.

The ingredients can vary. You can use leftover chicken, roasts, boiled meat, tuna, etc.

It's also tasty with a little catsup or mayonnaise. Don't go overboard on the ingredients. Be careful not to make a "heavy" dish; it should just be tasty and nutritious.

It's very nice served in halved tomatoes, lettuce leaves, or on toast. Make it!

## SIX-FLAVOR SALAD

*Ingredients for 2 servings:*

2 oz. tongue (fresh is better)
2 oz. lean prosciutto, cut into thin slices
2 oz. Gruyere cheese
2 oz. raw fennel
2 oz. celery
2 oz. raw carrots

**Condiments:**

2 teaspoons oil
the juice of half a lemon
salt
pepper
1 cup mayonnaise

**To Garnish:**

1 raw carrot
1 bunch parsley

Put the tongue slices together, roll like a cigar, and cut into thin strips. Do the same with the prosciutto. Also cut the cheese into strips (possibly with a food processor), also the celery and carrots, and finally slice the fennel with a sharp knife and then cut into strips.

Beat the oil together with the lemon juice, some salt, and pepper in a salad bowl. Combine the rest of the prepared ingredients, mix them, then add the mayonnaise, too.

Arrange the salad in a bowl, shape it into a dome, and decorate it with carrot slices cut into stars and parsley leaves. Refrigerate until ready to serve.

*Another version:* If you like spicy food add 1 or 2 tablespoons of Worcestershire sauce to the condiments. You can vary the presentation, besides, by putting the salad in bowls on top of green lettuce leaves.

★          ★          ★

## FRANKFURTER SALAD

*Ingredients for 2 servings:*

**1 package frankfurters**
**aurora sauce**
**mustard (optional)**

Cut the frankfurters and put them in a glass bowl. Season with aurora sauce plus a little mustard if you like.

## PROSCIUTTO MEDALLIONS IN GELATIN

*Ingredients for 2 servings:*

**5 oz. prosciutto**
**one yolk mayonnaise**
**2 tablespoons butter**
**2 oz. roasted peppers**
**gelatin for ½ qt.**
**2 tablespoons dry marsala**
**1 leaf laurel**

Prepare the gelatin according to package directions. I pass along the following three tips:

a) Put the gelatin in cold water in a pot and heat the pot, stirring continuously with a wooden spoon. Add a laurel leaf (it gets rid of the artificial taste).

b) When it boils, lower the heat and simmer. If it boils hard the gelatin will remain opaque.

c) After 4 minutes, turn off the heat. Add 1 tablespoon of dry marsala. It can be used for chicken in gelatin as well as various salad molds. When it thickens it is mashed with a fork, put into a syringe, and can be used to decorate any cold dish. In appropriate cylindrical molds (glasses can be used if you don't have the molds), put 2 tablespoons of the prepared gelatin.

While the gelatin is setting prepare the medallions. Put the slices of prosciutto on a cutting board (when you buy the prosciutto for this recipe ask that it be sliced a little thicker than usual). With a pasta cutter, cut prosciutto circles from the lean part of the slices (2 for each medallion that you want to make).

Whip the butter in a bowl until it mounds, then add the scraps of prosciutto, chopped or ground. Add a little salt and 1 teaspoon of dry marsala. Mix. Arrange the prosciutto medallions on the cutting board with the inferior sides up. Divide the mixture equally on each of the medallions. Spread the mixture on the circle and cover with another circle (it's easier to do than to describe!).

Take the gelatin molds. On top of the gelatin put a piece of roasted pepper and a bit of parsley. Then lay the medallion over the decoration. Cover it all with another 2 tablespoons of gelatin. Let it set. When the gelatin sets take a small pot of boiling water. Put the mold in the water for a second and then quickly unmold it in a serving platter by turning it upside down. Decorate the plate with the remaining peppers and parsley.

★          ★          ★

## PASTRY DOUGH

*Ingredients for about 10 pastry baskets or tarts:*

**3½ oz. flour**
**3 tablespoons butter**

Spread the flour on the table, add the butter and a little water, quickly mixing the dough. The dough should be soft. Work it with your hands for just a few minutes. Wrap it in a towel and leave if for about a half hour.

Roll out the dough very thin. Cover the metal forms previously greased. Poke with a toothpick and cover the bottom of the form with rice so the dough doesn't puff up while baking.

Put them in a hot oven for 10 minutes.

Cool, then take out the rice, remove the dough baskets from their forms, and fill them with Russian salad, Viennese pasta, prosciutto bits, etc.

★　　★　　★

## TUNA PÂTÉ

*Ingredients for 2 servings:*

**7 oz. potatoes**
**3½ oz. tuna**
**nutmeg**
**4 oz. butter**
**one yolk mayonnaise**
**various vegetables to decorate**
**1 oz. parsley**
**capers**

Boil the potatoes in cold salted water. In the meantime, prepare the mayonnaise.

When the potatoes are done mash them. Mash or blend the tuna together with the potatoes.

Add the butter, nutmeg, parsley, and capers (5 per person).

Mix until the mixture is well blended. Now give the mixture a form, a rectangle, or if you like, the form of a fish!

Cover the pâté with the mayonnaise, which should be liquid.

Decorate as you like.

★　　★　　★

## SANDWICHES

*Ingredients for 6 servings:*

**sliced bread or stale bread**
**pickled vegetables**
**hard-boiled eggs**
**salami**
**frankfurters, prosciutto**
**walnuts**
**capers**
**American cheese slices**
**catsup, green sause, aurora sauce, mayonnaise**
**anchovy sauce**

Slice the bread (excellent toasted), spread each slice with butter, or anchovy sauce, mayonnaise, green sauce, or aurora sauce. In each sandwich put some pickled vegetables, eggs, walnuts, cheese, prosciutto, etc.

• You'll have a fresh, appetizing, and nutritious dish.

These sandwiches are excellent for refreshing cold suppers.

★      ★      ★

## STOLEN SANDWICHES

*Ingredients for 2 servings:*

4  **slices bread**
1  **oz. dried mushrooms**
10  **walnuts**
1  **cup white sauce (1 oz. flour, 5 oz. butter, 1 oz. salt)**

Preheat the oven to 400°. Meanwhile, prepare the white sauce. When the white sauce is cooked, add the chopped mushrooms (previously soaked in hot water). Mix.

Take a slice of bread and spread a little white sauce with mushrooms on it. Do the same with the rest of the bread and white sauce. Sprinkle each slice of bread with some nuts.

Put the slices in the oven and let them get golden.

● Serve hot and you'll understand why they're called "stolen"!

## CREPE TORTE

*Ingredients for 6 servings:*

15 crepes
 1 bowl mayonnaise
   assorted cured meats (prosciutto, salami, coppa, cima, tongue, etc.)
   carrot salad
   chicory salad, cut very fine
   hard-boiled eggs
   chicken salad

*The ingredients can vary according to the imagination of the cook and the possible leftovers which he or she intends to make disappear in an elegant manner*

This can be considered a cold dish or an antipasto—anyway, an original dish. The preparation is simple: spread mayonnaise on the first crepe and fill it with one of the ingredients shown (cured meats, or chicory salad with some egg slices, etc.). Put the second crepe on top, spread with mayonnaise, fill; then go on to the third crepe, always spreading on the mayonnaise and continuing until the ingredients are used up and the torte reaches a respectable height. Garnish the top crepe with puffs of mayonnaise.

★    ★    ★

## EGGS WITH TUNA AND MUSHROOMS

*Ingredients for 2 servings:*

**2 eggs**
**2 oz. tuna**
**2 oz. mushrooms in oil**
***To decorate:* chicory or salad, lettuce or wild red chicory and radishes.**

Put 2 eggs in a small pot and cover with cold water. Heat. Cook the eggs for 7 minutes (from when the water begins to boil). Cool them. When they have cooled, shell them.

Cut the eggs in half. Remove the yolk. Take a vegetable grinder or chopper: put in 3 halves of the egg yolks together with the tuna and mushrooms (one half yolk is reserved).

Make a paste with these ingredients. Make 4 balls and put them in the hard-boiled egg whites. Shred the chicory and put it or the lettuce leaves or wild chicory on a serving platter.

Put the eggs on the bed of lettuce or chicory on the serving platter. Decorate the eggs by sprinkling grated egg yolk (the half reserved) over the filled eggs.

The grated egg yolk sprinkled over the eggs resembles mimosa blossoms.

★        ★        ★

## POACHED EGGS IN AURORA SAUCE

*Ingredients for 2 servings:*

2 **eggs**
2 **slices bread**
2 **tablespoons butter**
2 **tablespoons white sauce**
2 **tablespoons catsup**
4 **oz. milk**
1 **oz. flour**
   **anchovies**
   **vinegar**

Prepare the white sauce with 2 tablespoons of butter, 2 tablespoons of flour, and 4 oz. of milk. When the white sauce is cooked, add 2 tablespoons of catsup to it.

Butter the 2 slices of bread and put them in a hot oven to toast. Or toast them in the toaster. Heat a pan of salted water, add 2 tablespoons of vinegar, and boil. Crack the 2 eggs into the boiling water (they must be completely immersed).

Cook until the white solidifies. In this way you have poached eggs. Put the slices of toast on a plate and an egg on each slice. Decorate with hot aurora sauce and an anchovy fillet on each egg. It can serve as a hot antipasto or a new, tasty main course.

● This dish is not harmful to those who have a bad liver nor to those who inspire one.

# 2

# SOUP

*Julian Cream soup — Energizing Soup — Minestrone with Winter Vegetables — Blended Minestrone — Pressure Cooker Minestrone — Pasta and Beans — Vegetable Soup*

## JULIAN CREAM SOUP

*Ingredients for 2 servings:*

10½ oz. potatoes
 1 tablespoon butter
 2 cups milk
 1 onion, carrot, celery rib, some parsley, some basil
 7 oz. toasted bread
   rosemary
   sage
 2 oz. Parmesan cheese

Cook the potatoes in the milk. Chop all the herbs and vegetables and sauté them in the butter. Salt them and when they're cooked throw them in the pot with the milk and potatoes.

After everything is cooked, whip with an electric beater right in the pot. Add a little butter and Parmesan and serve with the toast.

● It's fabulous!

Be careful never to add pasta! It's incompatible with the milk

★　　　★　　　★

## ENERGIZING SOUP

*Ingredients for 6 servings:*

**6 egg yolks**
**6 tablespoons Parmesan cheese**
**6 tablespoons crushed bread**
**7 cups broth**

Prepare the broth (meat broth is better). If you want to use bouillon cubes put the pot on the heat, quickly add the cubes, and don't add salt.

When the broth is about to boil, prepare the egg yolks in a bowl together with the bread and the Parmesan: mix well and dilute with a little broth.

As soon as the broth boils, pour in the egg mixture beating well with a fork so lumps don't form. Bring to a boil again and serve.

● This is a very light soup, nutritious and especially suitable when you're in a hurry or when you have neither rice nor pasta.

## MINESTRONE WITH WINTER VEGETABLES

*Ingredients for 2 servings:*

2  **potatoes, carrots, onions, zucchini, tomatoes**
7  **oz. beans**
2  **oz. lentils**
3½ **oz. pumpkin**
2  **ribs celery**
1  **oz. parsley**
1  **bunch basil**
   **some sage and rosemary leaves**
3½ **oz. Swiss chard**
   **oil**
   **salt**
   **a pinch wild fennel seeds (optional)**
   ***In spring add:***
3½ **oz. eggplant, peas, fava beans, string beans**

Clean and wash the vegetables. If you like your minestrone vegetables cut into cubes, then cut them into cubes. Put all the ingredients in a pot, add salt and 2 tablespoons of olive oil and the fennel seed, and just enough water to cover the vegetables. Cover and bring to a boil.

When boiling occurs, lower the heat. Cook slowly at least 2 hours.

Turn off the heat and, if you like, add a pat of butter, a little Parmesan, and a sprinkle of pepper.

★      ★      ★

## BLENDED MINESTRONE

*Ingredients for 2 servings:*

2 **potatoes, carrots, onions, zucchini, tomatoes**
7 **oz. beans**
2 **oz. lentils**
3½ **oz. pumpkin**
2 **ribs celery**
1 **bunch parsley**
   **some sage and rosemary leaves**
3½ **oz. Swiss chard**
   **oil**
   **salt**
   **a pinch wild fennel seed (optional)**
   *In spring add:*
3½ **oz. peas, eggplant, fava beans, string beans**

Put all the vegetables in the pot whole, a regular pot, or a pressure cooker. The cooking time remains the same.

When the vegetables are cooked, before serving, blend them with an electric hand mixer or put them in the blender.

After blending the minestrone if the mixture is too liquidy, add toasted bread or pasta or rice (1 oz. per person) cooking it in the normal way.

★     ★     ★

## PRESSURE COOKER MINESTRONE

*Ingredients for 2 servings:*

2  potatoes, carrots, onions zucchini, tomatoes
7  oz. beans
2  oz. lentils
3½ oz. pumpkin
2  ribs celery
1  oz. parsley
1  bunch basil
   some sage and rosemary leaves
3½ oz. Swiss chard
   oil
   salt
   a pinch wild fennel seed (optional)
   *In spring add:*
3½ oz. eggplant, peas, fava beans, string beans

Put all the ingredients in a pressure cooker with salt and oil. Add very little water (don't cover the vegetables with it).

Heat to boiling, lower the heat to minimum, and cook 45 minutes.

Very little water is needed because it doesn't evaporate and if you use too much water your soup may be too watery.

Turn off the heat, let the steam escape, and season with butter, Parmesan cheese, and pepper.

★      ★      ★

## PASTA AND BEANS

*Ingredients for 6 servings:*

10½ oz. dried beans (17½ oz. if fresh — net weight, naturally, without the shells)
21 oz. spare ribs
1 pork bone (if possible the bone from prosciutto)
7 oz. pig skin
5 oz. smoked bacon
3 oz. per person (18 oz. in this case) fresh or dried pasta
1 sprig sage
garlic
oil
4 tablespoons flour
salt, as much as needed

In a pot with 6 full quarts of cold water, put the beans, pork bone, a sprig of sage, and salt.

Cook for 1 hour, add the spare ribs and pig skin (cleaned well).

In a pan put a clove of garlic, enough oil to cook the diced bacon, add 4 tablespoons of flour and let it brown for 10 minutes as when making white sauce.

Pour it all into the pot with the beans and cook over low heat at least 1 hour. Finally, add the pasta. This type of soup loves to be cooked so if you leave it cooking for even 3 hours (over low heat), it will be grateful and show you it's flavor!

• Pasta and beans is excellent when served not too hot, and if there is some left over, it's very good reheated, even with the pasta.

You'll know it's turned out well when your mixing spoon can stand straight up in the pot!

*Note:* The dried beans should be soaked in warm water overnight.

## VEGETABLE SOUP

*Ingredients for 2 servings:*

2 **potatoes, carrots, onions, zucchini, tomatoes**
7 **oz. beans**
2 **oz. lentils**
3½ **oz. pumpkin**
2 **ribs celery**
1 **oz. parsley**
1 **bunch basil**
   **some sage and rosemary leaves**
3½ **oz. Swiss chard**
   **oil**
   **salt**
   **a pinch wild fennel seed (optional)**
7  **oz. stale bread**
2  **oz. fontina, Parmesan, butter, pepper**
   *In spring add:*
3½ **oz. eggplant**
3½ **oz. peas**
3½ **oz. fava beans**
3½ **oz. string beans**

If you want to serve this soup in an original way, take a pan and in it put 2 ladles of prepared soup, then add a layer of toast, made in the toaster or fried in butter. Put some slices of Parmesan cheese on the bread. Continue in this manner until you fill the pan. It's best to end with bread, fontina, Parmesan, and a little soup.

Bake in a very hot oven at 400° for about 15 minutes.

# 3

# PASTA

*"Bigoli" Pasta with Anchovies — Mother-in-law Macaroni — Spinach Gnocchi — Paula's Sardinian Gnocchi — Lasagna Bolognese — Egg Pasta — Green Pasta — Pink Pasta — Noodles with Peas and Dairy Products — Pasta with Butter and Sage — Spaghetti, Coal Vendor's Style — Spaghetti with Mozzarella and Tomato — Spaghetti with Tomato and Tuna — Spaghetti with Fresh Tomato Sauce — Tortellini with Cream — Pasta with Pesto Genovese — Pesto Sauce Genovese — Tomato Sauce with Meat — Tomato Sauce.*

## "BIGOLI" PASTA WITH ANCHOVIES

*Ingredients for 4 servings:*

14 oz. "bigoli" spaghetti
7 oz. salted anchovies
2 oz. olive oil
1 clove garlic
   salt

Clean and remove the bones from the fish, then wash them well and dry them.

Heat a pot with plenty of salted water to boiling. Add the pasta when the water boils.

While the pasta is cooking, sauté the crushed garlic in the oil in a pan over mininum heat. When the garlic is golden, remove it. Add the anchovies to the oil, then mash them well with a fork. Cook without letting the oil boil.

Drain the pasta and season with the prepared sauce.

Mix and serve without cheese like all first course fish dishes.

*Note:* "Bigoli" pasta is not exclusive to Mantova because it is found in the oldest Venetian cooking: they are round, rather thick spaghetti, homemade on a press, which is the basic secret for the true success of this very tasty, even if simple dish.

In the old days this pasta was so highly valued that for a Mantovan to say "to go to bigoli" meant "to go to a good dinner."

Many families add chopped parsley and a little tuna to the sauce.

★    ★    ★

## MOTHER-IN-LAW MACARONI

*Ingredients for 2 servings:*

5 oz. pasta (penne rigate)
4 tablespoons tomato sauce
4 tablespoons cream
3½ oz. prosciutto
2 tablespoons Parmesan cheese
2 tablespoons pecorino cheese
2 tablespoons butter

Cook the pasta. Meanwhile, put the tomato sauce and heavy cream in a small saucepan and bring to a boil.

Drain the pasta, season with butter and the prepared sauce, and add the cheese and prosciutto cut into strips.

• Mothers-in-law continue their own competition with these little dishes. It's useless to be jealous, just copy their recipes. . . . Your husband will be less nostalgic.

★    ★    ★

## SPINACH GNOCCHI

*Ingredients for 4 servings:*

25 oz. spinach (2 lbs. if they have many stems and, therefore, a lot to discard)
 7 oz. ricotta
 7 oz. flour approximately
 5 spoonfuls grana padano cheese
 3 eggs
   nutmeg
   salt
   pepper

Boil the spinach, squeeze well, and pass through a sieve into a bowl.

Add the ricotta, which has also been passed through a sieve, 2 whole eggs plus 1 egg yolk, 5 spoonfuls of grana padano cheese, salt, pepper, and a pinch of nutmeg. Mix well with a wooden spoon and add enough flour to obtain a mixture that's not too soft.

Grease your hands with oil and make tiny balls the size of cherries, placing them in a floured dish.

Bring to a boil plenty of salted water and then carefully put in the gnocchi, mix slowly and boil for about 1 minute; don't let the water boil too hard.

• These spinach gnocchi are excellent with melted butter and Parmesan cheese or with tomato sauce. What an impression you'll make on your mother-in-law!

★     ★     ★

## PAULA'S SARDINIAN GNOCCHI

*Ingredients for 2 servings:*

5  oz. Sardinian gnocchi
3½ oz. canned beans
3½ oz. smoked bacon
   basil
   parsley
   onion
5  oz. peeled or fresh tomatoes
1  tablespoon grated pecorino cheese
1  tablespoon grated Parmesan cheese

Heat a pot with at least 1 quart of salted water to boiling. When the water boils, throw in the gnocchi and cook for 20 minutes.

In the meantime, dice the bacon, put it in a skillet, and brown it a little. Add 2 basil leaves, some parsley, and a chopped onion. Sauté.

Add fresh chopped or peeled tomatoes. Mix. Add salt and the boiled beans (drain the liquid from the can). Mix, and cook a few minutes.

Drain the gnocchi and season with this tasty sauce; add the cheeses, mix, and serve hot—then tell me that life isn't beautiful! . . .

★          ★          ★

## LASAGNA BOLOGNESE

*Ingredients for 2 servings:*

**10½ oz. fresh pasta**
   **tomato sauce**
**7  oz. fontina cheese**
   **white sauce**
**3½ oz. Parmesan cheese**

Prepare a very liquid white sauce; also prepare the tomato sauce. Slice the fontina cheese and grate the Parmesan.

Cut the fresh pasta into squares (2″ x 2″). Heat a pot with plenty of salted water.

When the water boils throw in 4-5 pieces of pasta and cook for 3 minutes. Remove the pasta, drain, and rinse under cold water. Lay the pasta pieces on a damp dish towel on the table.

In this way the pieces won't stick together and you'll have separate pieces to lay in the pan. Cook the pasta a little at a time. Having cooked half the pasta, take a baking pan. Put a little sauce on the bottom of the pan.

Put a layer of pasta in the pan. On top of the pasta put sauce, some Parmesan, some fontina cut into strips, and some white sauce. Prepare more pasta and continue to make layers (like the first). Top with the white sauce and bake in a hot oven at 500°. Let it brown and sit down pleased with yourself. After the baked pasta, if you wish, you can eat a slice of boiled meat with a salad and maybe a light fruit salad.

● Salad and fruit give you the vitamins needed for a sensible diet.

★      ★      ★

# Homemade Pasta

## EGG PASTA

*Ingredients for 2 servings:*

**5 oz. flour**
**1 egg**
**1 oz. semolina**
   **salt**

Combine the flour, egg, and salt. Work for a few moments with a fork and mix together well all the ingredients. If necessary, add a little warm water. The semolina, mixed with the flour, makes the dough very stiff, so you won't have a gooey table.

Having mixed the dough, go on to the mechanical work of rolling out a thin dough and cutting it however you like.

★　　　★　　　★

## GREEN PASTA

Prepare the same as for egg pasta, adding 1 oz. steamed spinach. Grind the spinach and add it to the pasta.

★　　　★　　　★

## PINK PASTA

Prepare the same as for egg pasta, adding ¼ oz. tomato paste to the normal pasta dough.

*Note:* If you like you can buy the fresh dough. Ask to have it rolled out very thin.

★　　　★　　　★

## NOODLES WITH PEAS AND DAIRY PRODUCTS

*Ingredients for 2 servings:*

2 tablespoons butter
1 sprig sage
1 oz. cream
1 oz. mascarpone cheese
3½ oz. natural peas (canned or fresh)
3½ oz. prosciutto
2½ oz. green noodles
2½ oz. yellow noodles
2 tablespoons Parmesan cheese

Sauté the sage in the butter, add the cream, and bring to a boil. Add the peas and lastly the mascarpone. Cook for 15 minutes. Cook the pasta, drain, and add the prosciutto cut into strips; add the sauce and the Parmesan.

Mix well. Good!

★     ★     ★

## PASTA WITH BUTTER AND SAGE

*Ingredients for 2 servings:*

5 oz. pasta
2 oz. butter
2 oz. Parmesan cheese
  sage

Cook the pasta in boiling, salted water with oil.

Melt the butter in a pan, add the sage, and sauté (don't burn it). Drain the pasta and season with the butter; discard the sage. Add the Parmesan.

★     ★     ★

## SPAGHETTI, COAL VENDOR'S STYLE

*Ingredients for 2 servings:*

5 oz. spaghetti
3½ oz. smoked bacon
1 egg yolk
2 tablespoons heavy cream
2 tablespoons pecorino cheese
2 tablespoons Parmesan cheese
  some pepper

Cook the spaghetti "al dente." Meanwhile, put the cheese in a bowl with the cream and egg yolk. Beat vigorously with a wooden spoon.

Slice the bacon and fry it in an iron skillet. It must become brown and crispy. Drain the spaghetti well and put it in the bowl with the cheese-cream-egg mixture.

Mix quickly and well, add the bacon and pepper, and eat this fabulous hodgepodge.

★　　★　　★

## SPAGHETTI WITH MOZZARELLA AND TOMATO

*Ingredients for 2 servings:*

5 oz. spaghetti
3½ oz. mozzarella
3½ oz. tomatoes

Cook the pasta. Prepare the tomatoes, peeling and chopping them. Slice the mozzarella.

Drain the pasta and return it to the pot where it cooked. Quickly add the mozzarella, mix, and heat over minimum heat for a few seconds so that the mozzarella will melt. Remove from the heat, add the raw, chopped tomatoes, mix, and serve.

• This is a light and nutritious pasta dish.

✱　　✱　　✱

## SPAGHETTI WITH TOMATO AND TUNA

*Ingredients for 2 servings:*

**5 oz. spaghetti**
**3½ oz. tuna**
**7 oz. fresh tomatoes**

Cook the pasta. Meanwhile peel the tomatoes and finely chop them as well as the tuna.

Drain the pasta and season with the tomatoes and tuna. More oil is not needed; the oil in the tuna is enough.

• It's light, tasty, and quick.

## SPAGHETTI WITH FRESH TOMATO SAUCE

*Ingredients for 2 servings:*

**5  oz. spaghetti**
**1  small bunch basil**
**1  small bunch parsley**
**2 garlic cloves**
**3½ oz. fresh plum tomatoes**
   **oil**
   **Parmesan cheese**

Cook the pasta. Meanwhile, peel the tomatoes—putting them in boiling water for a moment will make it easier.

Chop the tomatoes, basil, garlic, and parsley. Drain the pasta when it's "al dente." Add the tomatoes; mix. On top of the pasta put the parsley, garlic, and basil.

Separately, heat 4 tablespoons of olive, and when it's very hot pour it on the spaghetti. Cover the bowl of spaghetti for a moment with a lid. Mix and serve. The Parmesan cheese is optional.

• This sauce gives you the enormous advantage of eating the tomatoes and herbs raw and, therefore, full of vitamins. It's an enormous nutritional advantage. They are delicious!

★     ★     ★

## TORTELLINI WITH CREAM

*Ingredients for 2 servings:*

**For the filling:**
3 tablespoons of grated Parmesan cheese
2 tablespoons of butter
3½ oz. prosciutto
1 egg yolk
1 pinch salt
nutmeg

**For the pasta dough:**
7 oz. flour
1 egg

Finely chop the prosciutto. Whip the butter and add the prosciutto, the Parmesan, egg yolk, and nutmeg. Mix well.

This is the filling. Then make the egg pasta dough rolling it out rather thin.

In order for the tortellini to remain well sealed it's necessary to work the dough a little at a time. When you have a strip of dough ready, immediately cut circles about 1½ inches in diameter.

On each circle put some of the filling. Close by folding the circle in half sealing well the 2 ends forming the typical tortellini that you all know.

Continue in this manner with the rest of the filling and dough. If you don't want to make tortellini you can make "agnolotti."

Heat a pot with plenty of salted water. When the water boils throw in the tortellini and cook for 3-4 minutes.

★    ★    ★

## PASTA WITH PESTO GENOVESE

*Ingredients for 2 servings:*

5 oz. pasta
1 oz. tender green beans
2 medium potatoes
  pesto sauce Genovese
  grated pecorino cheese
  salt

Heat a pot with plenty of salted water; when it boils add the peeled, sliced potatoes and the cleaned and washed beans cut into 2 or 3 pieces.

When the vegetables are almost cooked add the pasta and as soon as it's ready ("al dente") drain it together with the potatoes and beans, reserving a ladleful of this water. Put the pasta and vegetables into a serving bowl.

## PESTO SAUCE GENOVESE

*Ingredients for 2 servings:*

16 basil leaves
 1 tablespoon pecorino cheese (not too sharp)
 1 tablespoon Parmesan cheese
 1 clove garlic
½ oz. pine nuts (pignoli)
  salt
½ glass olive oil

In the making of real pesto sauce it's important to use a marble mortar and a wooden pestle.

Delicately wash the basil leaves and drain well without crushing them, put them in the mortar, add the pine nuts that have been toasted in the oven, add the garlic and a pinch of salt (to retain the green color of the basil).

Begin by crushing the ingredients against the sides of the mortar with the pestle (not pounding them as is commonly done) gradually adding the 2 types of cheese that can vary according to your tastes.

Work until you obtain a green mixture. Then pour the mixture into a bowl and, continuing to mix with a wooden spoon, add ½ glass of oil a little at a time. Continue mixing until the mixture becomes creamy.

When you're ready to serve the pasta dilute the pesto with a spoonful of the pasta's cooking water. If the pesto is used for a minestrone, it's good to dilute it with a little broth, adding it then to the minestrone a few minutes before taking the minestrone from the heat. The Ligurians use "pesto" in various ways.

*Note:* I didn't have a classic mortar so I made it like this: I put the basil, garlic (without the sprout that makes it indigestible), the salt, toasted pine nuts, cheese, and oil in a blender. In one minute I have a fabulous pesto!

## TOMATO SAUCE WITH MEAT

*Ingredients for 2 servings:*

1½ oz. raw chopped meat (if you use cooked meat
        the sauce won't come as good because the
        meat has been depleted in the previous cook-
        ing)
1½ oz. sausage
1 rib celery
1 small bunch parsley
1 small bunch basil
1 small onion
1 sprig sage
1 sprig rosemary
1 glass wine
  oil
7 oz. fresh or canned, peeled tomatoes
1 package dried mushrooms (optional)

Wash and dry all the seasonings: finely chop them
(don't put them in a blender because then they won't
sauté on account of the water produced by the blender).

Sauté the herbs in the oil. Then add the chopped meat
and the sausage, brown them, and add salt (if you add salt
first it will cause water to come out of the vegetables and
the meat hindering the browning process). Mix with a
wooden spoon and add the wine. Let the wine evaporate
and, finally, add the dried mushrooms that have been
softened in hot water and chopped.

Mix and add the chopped tomatoes, mix, add a glass
of cold water, bring to a boil, and cover. Cook at least 1
hour—better yet 2 hours! This is the lord of Italian "ragu":
it must be made right so as not to lose its fame, envied by
all.

This sauce is laborious but it can be used for: pasta,
baked pasta, risotto, and potato gnocchi. You can use it to
reheat leftover roasted meat, meatballs, and eggs. You

can keep it in a closed container in the refrigerator for 1 week but it can easily be put in the freezer in small containers ready to use.

★ ★ ★

## TOMATO SAUCE

*Ingredients for 2 servings:*

**7 oz. fresh or canned, peeled tomatoes**
  **basil**
  **parsley**
  **onion**
  **sage**
  **celery**
  **rosemary**
  **salt**

Put the chopped tomatoes, salt, and all the other seasonings in a pot, and cook for 15 minutes without water.

Strain and if the juice is too watery let it thicken on the heat. When ready to serve add a little raw oil. It's excellent to season white rice and pasta and to make scrambled eggs.

● This is a light sauce, without fats, and can be kept in the refrigerator for a long time.

# 4

# RICE

*Rice with Mushrooms — Rice Fondue — Rice with Artichokes — Rice and Wild Chicory — Rice with Quail*

## RICE WITH MUSHROOMS

*Ingredients for 2 servings:*

5 oz. rice
1 package dried mushrooms
1 qt. broth
  Parmesan cheese
  oil
2 bouillon cubes

Put 1 quart of water and the 2 bouillon cubes into a pot. If you have beef broth, use that.

Put the dried mushrooms in a bowl and cover them with boiling water. Leave them in the water for 3 minutes. Remove the mushrooms, then squeeze and chop them.

In a skillet put 2 tablespoons of olive oil. Add the chopped mushrooms and sauté. Add the rice and sauté it with the mushrooms (2-3 minutes). Add some broth—just enough to cover the rice.

Mix with a wooden spoon and let the rice absorb the broth. When the broth has been completely absorbed by the rice, add more, mixing only when you add the broth. In this way the rice won't stick and you won't be forced to stir continuously.

The rice is cooked when it no longer absorbs any broth, usually after about 15 minutes. Remove from the heat, add the Parmesan, and serve.

Don't cover the rice while cooking.

★      ★      ★

## RICE FONDUE

Boil the rice in salted, boiling water for 15 minutes. Drain and add a few drops of oil and the fondue sauce.

Mix well and serve (excellent when served in pastry baskets or tarts).

★      ★      ★

## RICE WITH ARTICHOKES

*Ingredients for 2 servings:*

5 oz. rice
2 tablespoons butter
1 oz. Parmesan cheese (2 tablespoons)
2 artichokes
2 cups broth
   beef and chicken bouillon cubes

In a saucepan put ½ chicken bouillon cube and ½ beef bouillon cube. Add 2 cups of water and bring to a boil.

Meanwhile, clean the artichokes and cut them into thin slices. Put the butter in a pot, add the artichokes, and sauté. Then add the rice and mix.

Add the hot broth a little at a time. It's not necessary to stir continuously; just stir when you add the broth. After 15 minutes the rice is "al dente" but it's fine like this.

Remove from heat, add the Parmesan, and serve hot.

• It's very tasty and digestible.

★      ★      ★

## RICE AND WILD CHICORY

*Ingredients for 2 servings:*

**5 oz. rice**
**1 medium onion**
**3½ oz. wild chicory**
**1 qt. broth**
   **a sprinkle of dry white wine**
   **oil**
   **butter**
   **Parmesan cheese**

Put the oil, butter, and finely chopped onion in a pot. Sauté the onion, add the washed and cut chicory (cut the same as for salad), and fry until a creamy mixture is obtained.

Add the rice, let it absorb some flavor, then add the white wine. Let the wine evaporate, then add the hot broth a little at a time, stirring constantly, like the usual risotto.

Add the Parmesan and serve.

● The color is a little strange but the taste is excellent! Like "Rice with Red Wine" or "Rice with Mushrooms": it's a real surprise!

★    ★    ★

## RICE WITH QUAIL

*Ingredients for 4 servings:*

**5 oz. rice**
**3½ oz. butter**
**4 quail, plucked and cleaned**
**1 onion**
**4 thin slices of lard or bacon**
**5 spoonfuls Parmesan cheese**
**1 qt. white meat broth**
**½ ("generous") glass dry white wine**
  **salt**
  **pepper**
  *If you like:*
**1 sprig rosemary**
**1 clove garlic**
  **some sage**

This recipe can be a complete course and, followed by cheese and fruit, constitutes a complete meal. If this is to be the case, buy 8 quail instead of 4 and make sure they are plump.

If necessary, scorch the quail to remove their down, make sure they are thoroughly cleaned, wash them well, and let them drain (or dry with a cloth). Inside each one put a pinch of salt and its liver. Then lay them down and wrap in a slice of lard or bacon, tying them with some thread.

When they're all ready, brown them in a pot large enough to hold them all and 1 oz. of butter. Continue browning, adding a little less than ½ glass of white wine, a little at a time (in the ingredients ½ "generous" glass of wine is listed; the little wine that remains from the "generous" half-glassful will be used to prepare the rice). When the wine evaporates add salt and pepper and continue cooking over moderate heat, turning frequently.

If you like, add some sage, a sprig of rosemary, and a crushed garlic clove. Immediately after starting the quail, sauté the finely sliced onion in a pot in half the remaining butter, over moderate heat (it mustn't get brown). Add the rice and, stirring constantly, sauté it for 1 or 2 minutes, then add the rest of the wine.

When the wine has evaporated, sprinkle with a ladleful of hot broth, stirring constantly. Continue cooking, adding more broth when needed and stirring constantly until the rice is cooked (be careful not to overcook it). Scald a serving platter with boiling water. Five minutes before turning off the rice, add the rest of the butter and about half the grated cheese.

Arrange the rice on the hot platter, put the quail on top (remove the thread), sprinkle with the gravy in the pot (if necessary dilute it with a spoonful of hot broth), and serve accompanied by the rest of the cheese.

Needless to say if you add some porcini mushrooms to the gravy (preferably small and compact), the results will be much much better.

# 5

## MEAT

*Grilled Sausage — Fantastic Meat Kabobs — Grilled Beef Steak — Kabobs — Braised Beef with Red Wine — Braised Beef with Red Wine in a Pressure Cooker — Rabbit in Wine — Guinea Hen in Foil — Meat Slices, Alba Style — Meat Slices Pizzaiola — Meat Slices, Roman Style — Meat Slices with Cheese — Roast Meat Slices — Chicken Breasts with Cream — Chicken Breasts with Cream and Mushrooms — Hunter's Style Chicken — Chicken with Olives — Cockerel Kabobs — Quail with Milk — Stew, My Way*

## Kinds of Meat

The nutritive value of meat and its importance in the diet of children and young people is such a highly debated subject that it's worth dwelling upon.

Meat is subdivided into three main groups:
a) *red meat:* beef, horsemeat, pork, lamb, etc.;
b) *white meat:* veal, rabbit, poultry, fish;
c) *dark meat:* wild boar and game in general.

*Digestibility of Meat:* naturally, each of these three groups has a different digestibility, so much so that the best one for convalescents and those with weak stomachs is white meat. In order for meat to be tasty and digestible it must be "soft," that is, the animal must have been killed 24 or 36 hours before.

Which is best? That depends on the circumstances: each meat is selected on the basis of the dish intended, the person for whom it's prepared, the climate where you live, etc.

Not only the type of meat must be selected but also the cut. Do you have to make boiled meat? It's advisable to decide if you want good boiled meat or a good broth. If you want a *good broth* put the meat in from the beginning and add the vegetables (celery, carrots, onion, rosemary, cloves); if you want *good boiled meat* add the meat when the water, already salted and flavored, boils.

## Ways of Cooking Meat

### Broiling and Boiling

With *broiling* the nutrients remain in the meat protected by the light crust that is formed by direct contact with the flame.

With *boiling* a good part of the meat's nutrients are left in the liquid in which it's immersed or which is added to it during cooking.

Belonging to the first group are the true roasted meats, that is, those broiled in the oven, grilled on a barbecue or a spit, or the so-called "dead" roasts because they get their protective crust by browning in a pot or pan.

To the second group belong: the boiled meats, braised meats, and steamed meats.

To these two principal groups another very important one is added: fried meats.

## Cuts of Meat

*For roasted or broiled meats:* fillet mignon, sirloin, rib, rump, or top sirloin can be used for steaks or, in larger pieces, roasts.

For roast beef use rolled rump roast since it is very tender.

When buying fillet mignon be sure that you're given the "heart" of the fillet, that is, the central part.

*For boiling:* if you want broth together with a good piece of boiled meat ask for some brisket or top sirloin. If you want broth but don't care about the boiled meat, ask for ribs.

*For cutlets:* rump, top sirloin, or top round is preferable.

*For stew:* shinbone meat is used.

*For steaming:* use eye round, bottom round, or shoulder.

## Grilled Meats

**Practical advice from an expert . . . modestly speaking!**

You can proceed, based on the cooking times listed in the table on page 211, to begin your own grilling experience. There are, however, other rules to remember.

In the first place, the meat must be as dry as possible when it's put on the grill. If it has been marinating, as called for in many recipes, it is better to dry it perfectly. The marinade itself, generally made with oil, lemon juice, and other aromatic herbs, will be delicately brushed on the meat while cooking in such a way that the surface remains soft while care is taken that it doesn't drip into the fire, burning and giving off a bad smell.

Salt and pepper are added at the last minute, better yet after it's removed from the fire. Salt, in particular, causes excessive softening of the meat's surface neutralizing the protective external film and consequently, losing the juices.

The fire: in the case of a barbecue grill, charcoal is required, but the temperature of the fire is very important and it's necessary to stress some things. First of all, the surface area of the red-hot coals should be at least twice as large as the cooking food. Also, they should be placed in the brazier in such a way as to make the sides a little higher than the center. This will serve to radiate heat in a winding manner, without dispersing it. Finally, a basic rule is never to touch the fire while a piece of meat is cooking. Any change in the intensity of the heat, even if to revive the coals, has a negative effect on the meat. When a steak has begun to cook, even if you realize that the fire is not at its best, it's better to leave it alone. It's less damaging than blowing on it or moving it with a poker.

# Kabobs

In the vast panorama of possibilities offered in outdoor cooking, kabobs have become an imposing force in the last few years here, because of the extremely varied approach they allow and their great practical preparation. Therefore, it's necessary to linger over them for a moment.

Kabobs can be prepared using metal skewers made for this purpose, easily found in any size and shape, or by using wooden skewers in a more orthodox manner. Here you have, however, the problem of smell: you must be careful not to use wood with a very pungent flavor because while cooking in direct contact with the food it can disastrously transfer some of its taste to the food. If you can find it, it's advisable to gather a good quantity of heather and then, patiently, make skewers with a sharp knife. In fact, heather, according to many gourmets, is the only plant totally devoid of smell and, what's more, respectful of the flavor of food.

A discussion about the preparation of kabobs would be too long. There's no limit to imagination, and this, too, is one of the reasons for their success.

Secondly, the possible combinations are practically limitless: we can use every kind of meat or giblets, from liver to kidneys and heart, every kind of fish, mollusks, mushrooms, vegetables, cheeses, interposing each ingredient with aromatic herbs. In some meat kabobs, for example, the meat is interposed with pieces of lemon rind, which in cooking acquire an absolutely unique flavor.

The third and final advantage kabobs offer is that they are especially suited to cooking on a grill, and are, therefore, simple to prepare, easy to make, and easy to

## Grilled Meat and Kabobs (Cooking Times)

| | thickness | fire | rare | medium | well done |
|---|---|---|---|---|---|
| **beef** | | | | | |
| steak | 1 inch | high | 4 min. | 6 min. | 10 min. |
| rib | 1½ inches | high | 7 min. | 10 min. | 15 min. |
| round | 1½ inches | high | 6 min. | 10 min. | 15 min. |
| kabobs | — | medium | 6 min. | 8 min. | 10 min. |
| hamburgers | 1 inch | high | 6 min. | 8 min. | 10 min. |
| **veal** | | | | | |
| cutlets | ½ inch | medium | — | 4 min. | 6 min. |
| chops | 1 inch | medium | — | 9 min. | 12 min. |
| kabobs | — | medium | — | 10 min. | 12 min. |
| large pieces | — | medium | — | 15 min. each 11 oz. | — |
| **pork** | | | | | |
| steak | 1 inch | low | — | — | 10 min. |
| chops | 1 inch | low | — | — | 10 min. |
| large pieces | — | low | — | — | 15 min. each 11 oz. |
| kabobs | — | low | — | 8 min. | 11 min. |
| **lamb** | | | | | |
| chops | ½ inch | low | 3 min. | 4 min. | 6 min. |
| kabobs | — | low | — | 6 min. | 8 min. |
| haunch | — | low | — | 25 min. each 2 lbs. | — |
| **poultry** | | | | | |
| whole chicken on skewer | — | medium | — | 35 min. | — |
| chicken pieces | — | medium | — | 35 min. | — |
| pigeon | — | medium | — | 25 min. | — |
| duck | — | high | — | 35 min. | — |
| **game** | | | | | |
| quail | — | high | — | 12 min. | — |
| thrush | — | high | — | 10 min. | — |
| birds | — | high | — | 5 min. | — |
| partridge | — | high | — | 25 min. | — |
| **fish** | | | | | |
| whole | 1½ inches | medium | — | 15 min. | — |
| whole | ¾ inch | medium | — | 6 min. | — |
| fillets | — | medium | — | 5 min. | — |
| slices | ¾ inch | medium | — | 6 min. | — |

eat. When eating outdoors, a slight departure from traditional table manners is permitted. So there's nothing better than kabobs to relish—without dishes, forks, and knives—the more genuine and inviting flavor of the simplest and healthiest type of cooking.

## GRILLED SAUSAGE

*Ingredients for 6 servings:*

**12 small sausages
(cooking time: about 15 minutes)**

Cut the sausages in half lengthwise leaving them attached on one end.

Heat the grill. Arrange the sausage on the grill with the cut side down first (so that they don't curl). Brown them well and serve hot.

★    ★    ★

## FANTASTIC MEAT KABOBS

*Ingredients for 6 servings:*

**21 oz. beef fillet
14 oz. sausage
12 mushroom caps (approximately)
12 small tomatoes
12 small onions
 1 clove garlic
   oil
   salt**

Cut the sausage and meat into chunks.

Wash and dry the mushrooms and tomatoes; clean the onions.

Using metal skewers alternate 2 pieces of meat, 2 pieces of sausages, 2 mushrooms, 2 tomatoes, 2 onions and continue in this way until all the ingredients have been used up.

Mince the garlic and add it to enough oil and a pinch of salt. Brush this mixture on the kabobs and cook on the barbecue grill.

While they are cooking, turn them frequently and brush them with more of the oil mixture, until they are well cooked and crispy.

★ ★ ★

## GRILLED BEEF STEAK

*Ingredients for 6 servings:*

**6 beef steaks, 7 oz. each**
**1 lemon**
**oil**
**salt**
**pepper**
**(cooking time: about 15 minutes plus marinating time)**

Prepare a marinade with a few tablespoons of oil, lemon juice, and a pinch of pepper; put the steaks in and let them marinate for 1 hour.

Heat the grill well. Drain the steaks of their marinade, put them on the grill, and cook them over rather high heat turning them just once: they should be well browned on the outside and juicy inside. Add salt only after cooking and serve them hot.

The same recipe can be used fo.· pork (fillet) and chicken or turkey breasts.

● Meat made like this is very tasty and easy to digest.

★ ★ ★

## KABOBS

*Ingredients for 2 servings:*

**3½ oz. chicken breast**
**3½ oz. turkey breast**
**3½ oz. frankfurters**
**3½ oz. smoked bacon**
**some sage leaves**
**wooden skewers about 8 inches long**
**pitted olives**
**pepper**
**sage**

Cut the meat, frankfurters, and bacon into chunks.

Take a skewer and thread a piece of chicken, an olive, a piece of turkey, a piece of frankfurter, a piece of bacon, and sage. Continue in this manner until the ingredients are all used up. Put a sheet of aluminum foil in a roasting pan.

Put the kabobs in the pan; add salt and pepper. Put them in a hot oven at 400° for 15 minutes. Use no condiments.

• You'll have tasty, light, and appetizing meat.

## BRAISED BEEF WITH RED WINE

*Ingredients for 2 servings:*

14 oz. lean beef
   parsley
   sage, rosemary, laurel, garlic
   onion, carrot, celery
   some flour
16 oz. red wine (barolo or barbera)
   olive oil
   some butter
   cinnamon
   cloves
   juniper berries
   pepper

To make good braised beef with red wine you need a piece of lean meat, from the leg section near the rump.

Chop the parsley, sage, rosemary, garlic, laurel, onion, carrot, and celery. Put some oil and some butter in a pot. Coat the meat with flour and brown it together with the vegetables and herbs.

Brown the meat on all sides, add salt, then add the cinnamon, cloves, pepper, and wine. Continue cooking, covered for 3 or 4 hours.

If you like you can put it in the oven, but in this case also the pot must be covered because the wine contains alcohol, which evaporates rapidly. To check the cooking, taste the gravy and add salt if needed.

Let it cool, slice the meat, put the slices in a baking dish, and cover with its own gravy, which should be quite thick.

*A few tricks:*

a) Barolo wine is expensive; you can remedy the situation without your guests knowing by using barbera wine to which you have added a shot of rum for every quart of wine.

b) If you grind the vegetables before cooking with the proper appliance, you won't have to blend them at the end of cooking.

c) If the gravy is too watery, you can thicken it by adding an egg yolk, mixing vigorously and then reheating over minimum heat. The egg will coagulate and thicken the gravy in a few seconds.

d) If you want to have a tasty braised beef, you must always be smart enough to cut the meat and cover it with its own gravy at least 2 hours before serving. When you're ready to serve simply put it in the oven for a few minutes.

★        ★        ★

## BRAISED BEEF WITH RED WINE IN A PRESSURE COOKER

*Ingredients for 2 servings:*

**same as previous recipe**

Put the oil and butter in a pressure cooker, add the meat (after coating it with flour), brown it, add salt, spices, and half the wine (because the liquid doesn't evaporate in a pressure cooker).

When the steam escapes from the valve on the pressure cooker continue cooking for 45 minutes. Continue as in the previous recipe.

★        ★        ★

## RABBIT IN WINE

*Ingredients for 2 servings:*

14 oz. rabbit cut into pieces
   onion, celery, carrot, basil, rosemary
 4 cloves
   cinnamon
   pepper
   oil
   flour
16 oz. red wine (barolo or barbera)

Put the rabbit in a glass bowl. Add the vegetables and spices.

Cover it all with the wine. Let it marinate overnight. When ready to cook the rabbit, take it out of the wine and coat each piece with flour.

Put a little oil in a pan (one that can go in the oven), and brown the rabbit pieces. When they are golden brown, salt them on both sides.

Add the vegetables and spices that you have put in the wine with the rabbit, and brown them. Then add the wine in which the meat marinated and bring to a boil. When it boils put the pan in a preheated oven at 475°.

Bake for 45 minutes. This way the meat cooks well, not dry, and you don't have to continually turn it or anything else.

● It's a fabulous dish, extremely simple. You can serve it with mashed potatoes, polenta, or other vegetables. If some gravy remains you can use it to make a good risotto.

Here's a secret just for you: Barolo wine is expensive. If you want barbera wine to taste the same, put 2 tablespoons of dry rum in every quart of barbera. You can also cook hare, pheasant, or a piece of beef (tenderloin, round, rib) in this manner.

★     ★     ★

## GUINEA HEN IN FOIL

*Ingredients for 4 servings:*

1 **guinea hen, 2½ - 3 lbs.**
2 **sprigs rosemary**
1 **sprig sage**
1 **tablespoon oregano**
2 **oz. butter**
  **salt**
  **pepper**
  **aluminum foil**
  **string**

Pluck, clean, and scorch the guinea hen; cut off the feet, clip the wings, cut off the head, wash and dry it with a clean cloth.

In a cup blend together 1 oz. of butter with half the oregano and a pinch of salt. Use this mixture to stuff the hen (first salt the interior of the hen), then tie the hen with some string.

Season the outside also with salt, pepper, and oregano; then put a few sage and rosemary leaves between the wings and legs.

Abundantly grease a sheet of aluminum foil with butter. Put the hen in the center. Wrap it up, sealing it inside.

Put the wrapped hen in a preheated 525° oven and cook for 45 minutes. When ready to serve take the hen out of the foil and cut it into 6 portions. Season with the juice in the foil.

Serve with French fries, spinach with butter, artichokes, etc.

## MEAT SLICES, ALBA STYLE

*Ingredients for 2 servings:*

2 veal cutlets sliced thin (about 3 oz. each)
1 porcini mushroom about 1 oz. or an equal amount
   of cultivated mushrooms
1 oz. Parmesan cheese
1 lemon
   oil, as much as needed
   salt
   pepper

Put the cutlets in a deep, oval dish and add salt and pepper. Add the juice of 1 lemon and a little olive oil. Slice the mushrooms and Parmesan and put them on top of the meat.

Let it remain like this for 4-5 hours.

This is an excellent antipasto: a good cold dish, tasty and nutritious and also easy to digest.

★    ★    ★

## MEAT SLICES PIZZAIOLA

*Ingredients for 2 servings:*

2 cutlets, about 3½ oz. each
4 fresh plum tomatoes or canned, peeled tomatoes
   basil, parsley, celery, onion, carrot, rosemary
3½ oz. fontina cheese
1 pinch oregano
2 capers
   dry white wine
   oil
   flour

Finely chop all the seasonings, sauté them in the oil (the oil and seasonings are put in the pan at the same time), coat the meat with flour, and add it to the pan with the seasonings.

Brown the meat together with the seasonings, then add salt and a little white wine. Let the wine evaporate, add the chopped tomatoes, and cook 2 or 3 minutes. Add the slices of fontina, the capers, and the oregano. Cover the pan and cook for 5 minutes.

● It's tasty and easy, but you must follow the recipe because it can also be disappointing.

This procedure can also be used in cooking chicken breasts or a whole, cut chicken. In this case you must cook it at least 45 minutes. It's very good also using turkey breast, hamburgers, quail, pheasant, and guinea hen.

★　　　★　　　★

**MEAT SLICES, ROMAN STYLE**

*Ingredients for 2 servings:*

2　slices veal for beef, about 3½ oz. each
4　slices prosciutto or bacon
　　sage
2　tablespoons butter
　　toothpicks

Cut each slice of meat into 4 pieces. Also cut the prosciutto or bacon. Take a piece of meat; put a piece of prosciutto or bacon on top of the meat and another under the piece of meat. Do the same with the sage leaves, then hold it all together with a toothpick.

Melt the butter in a skillet, add the meat, and brown on both sides. Add salt, but just a little because the prosciutto or bacon is salty. The slices don't need to cook more than 5 minutes.

• If you substitute liver for the meat you will have an equally good and nutritious dish.

★    ★    ★

## MEAT SLICES WITH CHEESE

*Ingredients for 2 servings:*

**2 slices meat about 3½ oz. each**
**4 oz. fontina cheese**
**2 tablespoons butter**
   **some capers**

Put the butter or oil in a skillet (butter is more suited) and let it heat a little. Add the meat and brown it on both sides, then add salt. Add the sliced fontina, add the capers, cover, and cook over low heat for 5 minutes. The longer they cook the tougher they'll be. The meat is 3½ oz. but remember that you are adding the cheese. Chicken or turkey cutlets can also be cooked in this way.

## ROAST MEAT SLICES

*Ingredients for 2 servings:*

**4  slices rabbit fillet**
**pepper**
**salt**
**rosemary**

Put a sheet of aluminum foil in a baking pan. Put the meat slices on the foil, add salt, pepper, and some rosemary or oregano.

Add condiments. Put all in a hot oven for 10 minutes (400°).

The same recipe can be used for: pork (fillet), chicken or turkey cutlets, and veal or beef cutlets.

● Meat made like this is very tasty and easy to digest.

★      ★      ★

## CHICKEN BREASTS WITH CREAM

*Ingredients for 2 servings:*

**2  slices chicken breasts**
**sage**
**butter**
**3½ oz. cream**

Put the butter and sage in a pan and sauté. Add the chicken, brown, add salt, and then add the cream. Bake in a hot oven at 475° for about 15 minutes.

★      ★      ★

## CHICKEN BREASTS WITH CREAM AND MUSHROOMS

*Ingredients for 2 servings:*

**7 oz. chicken fillet**
**1½ oz. butter**
**1 sprig sage**
**1 small glass dry white wine**
**7 oz. cream**
**3½ oz. porcini mushrooms**
    **or**
**½ oz. dried mushrooms**
    **salt**

Cut the chicken breasts into pieces. Put half the butter and some sage in a skillet.

Brown the chicken, then add salt and the white wine. Let the wine evaporate and add the cream. Cover and cook over low heat for 20 minutes. While the chicken is cooking, put the rest of the butter and a few sage leaves in a pan, add the cleaned, washed and sliced mushrooms, sauté, and add salt.

Add the mushrooms to the chicken and cook together over low heat 15 minutes more.

● You'll have a stupendous, delicious, and nutritious dish.

As a side dish you can serve artichokes in butter or raw in a salad and fried or mashed potatoes.

It's also excellent with polenta which makes it a complete course.

To complete such a meal all you need is a fresh fruit salad.

## HUNTER'S STYLE CHICKEN

*Ingredients for 2 servings:*

14 oz. chicken
 7 oz. fresh or canned, peeled tomatoes
 1 rib celery
 1 pinch parsley, 1 pinch basil
 1 sprig rosemary, 1 sprig sage
 1 piece onion
 1 laurel leaf
 4 tablespoons olive oil
 1 small glass dry white wine
   salt

Clean the chicken, scorch it to remove the down, wash it, and cut it into pieces (or have the butcher cut it).

Put the oil in a skillet along with the chopped seasonings. Add the chicken pieces. Sauté the chicken and seasonings together. When they are browned, add salt and the wine. Let the wine evaporate and then add the chopped tomatoes.

Mix and cover. Cook over very low heat for at least 45 minutes.

I prefer to sauté the chicken first and then continue cooking it in the oven. This method is more suitable and less trouble. It's less likely to burn, and you'll use less gas.

Certainly, the oven must be at 400° and the skillet must be one that can also be used in the oven. In the oven, bake the chicken for at least 1 hour. It's excellent.

• You can also cook rabbit, quail, goat ribs, pork roast, and turkey legs in the same way.

When it's good, it's good.

★      ★      ★

## CHICKEN WITH OLIVES

*Ingredients for 2 servings:*

**14 oz. chicken (meat with bones is always calcu-
   lated about double that without bones)**
 **4 tablespoons oil**
 **7 oz. black olives**
 **1 glass dry marsala**
   **salt**

Clean the chicken, scorch it, wash and dry it, and cut it into pieces (it cooks better and is easier to serve and eat).

Put the oil in a skillet, add the chicken browning it well on all sides, salt it, and add the olives and marsala. Lower the heat to minimum, cover, and cook for at least 45 minutes.

• This chicken dish, too, is excellent cooked in the oven. It is put into the oven after browning, salting, and adding the olives and marsala.

*Note:* All the chicken dishes mentioned here I serve like this: I cook the chicken according to the recipe, I make a normal polenta. When it's cooked I put it in a circular pan with a hole in the middle (ring shaped) and leave the polenta to set in the pan taking its form. Then before serving I put the pan with the polenta in the oven at 400° for about 15 minutes.

I unmold the warm polenta on a large round platter. In the hole in the middle I put the gravy from the chicken and I put the chicken pieces all around and bring it to the table in this marvelous way.

I have a complete course that I can prepare and still sit calmly at the table like a guest.

It's easy to make dinner an occasion to enjoy the company of others without confusing or troubling anyone. Great, right?

✱          ✱          ✱

## COCKEREL KABOBS

*Ingredients for 4 servings:*

1　**cockerel about 2 lbs.**
7　**oz. lard**
　　**sage**
　　**salt**
　　**pepper**
　　**extra-virgin olive oil**

Scorch the cockerel, clean it, wash and dry it, and cut it into pieces.

Take a skewer, one for the oven if you have it, or else buy wooden skewers (long and strong).

Slice the lard and cut the slices into pieces.

Remove the sage leaves (you need fresh sage with large leaves). Take the skewer and thread a piece of lard, a sage leaf, and a piece of cockerel, then lard, sage, and meat, etc. until all the ingredients are used. If you have wooden skewers one probably won't be enough; you'll have to make 2 kabobs.

When you have finished this, take white sewing thread and fasten the meat passing the thread from one end to the other. Fasten the meat well.

Now take a pot (choose one that can go in the oven), put in some olive oil, add the kabobs, and brown on all sides.

When they are well browned, add salt and pepper, cover the pot, and put it in a preheated oven at 400°. Cook for at least 1 hour. If you have a rotisserie, cook it for at least 1½ hours.

You can serve the kabobs as they are or you can remove the meat and put it on a serving platter. Accompany with roasted potatoes and artichokes.

• This is a dish that will insure a festive atmosphere and smell.

★　　　★　　　★

## QUAIL WITH MILK

*Ingredients for 2 servings:*

**2 quail**
**1 sprig sage**
**2 tablespoons butter**
   **dry white wine**
**2 cups milk**

Scorch the quail to remove any down. Clean them. Wash and dry them.

Using a skillet suitable for the oven, put in the butter, sage, and the quail. Brown the quail well. Then salt them and add a sprinkle of dry white wine.

Let the wine evaporate and add the milk. Bring to a boil and put the skillet in a preheated oven at 475°. Cook until the quail are well done and the milk is almost completely evaporated.

• The meat will be tender and very digestible because the milk neutralizes the acids in the meat.

This recipe can be used also with chicken, roasts, guinea hen, squab, etc.

★      ★      ★

**STEW, MY WAY**

*Ingredients for 6 servings:*

**7 oz. beef**
**7 oz. chicken**
**7 oz. pork**
**10½ oz. sausage**
   **celery, carrots, onions**
   **sage, rosemary, parsley, basil**
   **laurel**
**7 cloves**
   **cinnamon**
**17½ oz. tomatoes, fresh or canned**
**1 glass dry white wine**
   **salt, oil, butter**

Chop the sage, rosemary, parsley, and basil and sauté them in oil and butter. After you have sautéed them add salt and ½ glass of white wine. Let the wine evaporate, then add the tomatoes and continue cooking over very low heat.

Meanwhile, cut the assorted meats and sausage into chunks being careful to keep the different types separate from one another. Put some oil and butter in a pot. Taking the beef first, coat it with flour and brown each piece, then put it in one corner of the pot. Coat the pork with flour, brown it, and then put it next to the beef. Coat and brown the chicken and finally the sausage without coating it with flour.

It's easy to understand that the first one in the pot is the one that needs to be cooked longer and so on for the rest of the meat.

Putting the already browned meat aside in the pot is a trick to avoid using 2 pots when a relatively limited quantity is used.

Now, when everything has browned, add salt, then add ½ glass of wine, 6 or 7 cloves, a pinch of cinnamon, and a laurel leaf.

Pour into the pot with the meat the gravy previously prepared, mix, cover, and cook over low heat 45-60 minutes. It's even better if you put the pot, uncovered, in the oven at medium heat (the ideal temperature is that which allows for constant simmering as over minimum heat on the top of the stove).

• This is a spendid, tasty dish, rich in nutrients. You can serve it with polenta, mashed potatoes, or whatever you prefer. When it's half cooked you can even add 21 oz. of raw cubed potatoes. You'll have a complete course.

It keeps well even in the freezer up to 6 months.

# 6

## FISH

*Bass in Foil — Shrimp Cocktail — Roast Fish — Fried Fish — Steamed Mackerel — Seafood Salad — Sole in White Wine — Stuffed Weakfish*

### BASS IN FOIL

*Ingredients for 2 servings:*

**1 bass about 14 oz.**
**oil**
**parsley**
**laurel**
**onion**
**basil**
**cloves**
**cinnamon stick**

Clean and wash the bass. Wash and chop the herbs.

Open up the bass and add salt internally; also put the chopped herbs inside. Add a few cloves, some pepper, cinnamon, and olive oil.

Take a sheet of aluminum foil and grease it with oil. Put the bass on the foil, salt the outside of the fish, and wrap it securely in the foil.

Put the foil package in a preheated oven at 400°. Cook it for 20 minutes.

To my mind, this method of cooking is the best because it allows the fish to brown well while remaining tender and tasty and the kitchen doesn't smell of fish. It's truly a surprise package.

This method of cooking is good for trout, red mullet, and also slices of whiting and dentex, etc. In the case of fish pieces or fillets it's obvious that the herbs are put over each slice of fish and then each slice is wrapped in foil.

★　　　★　　　★

**SHRIMP COCKTAIL**

*Ingredients for 2 servings:*

**10½ oz. shrimp**
 **lettuce**
 **salt**
 ***For the dressing:***
**½ cup mayonnaise**
**½ glass cream**
**½ tablespoon catsup**
**½ tablespoon Worcestershire sauce**

Cook the shrimp in boiling, salted water, drain and cool, then remove shell.

Select the most tender leaves of lettuce, wash and dry them, and use them to line 2 crystal cups.

Make the dressing with the mayonnaise, cream, catsup, and Worcestershire sauce, and taste it; if necessary, enrich it according to your taste, remembering that the dressing must be very tasty to contrast with the sweetness of the shrimp.

Add the shrimp, mix, and spoon them into the cups.

Keep in the refrigerator until ready to serve.

You can also use precooked shrimp.

Use the same procedure for seafood salad—whether fresh or canned — cooked and ready to season.

● They look good and proclaim you a rather rare host!

★      ★      ★

# Cooking Roast Fish

Roast fish can be baked in the oven or made on the grill. Whichever way you choose, after having cleaned the fish as usual, put it in a plate an hour or two before cooking and season with some parsley, pepper, and laurel, then sprinkle with oil.

Don't add either lemon or salt.

Whether cooking in the oven or on a grill, when the fish is a certain weight you need to make diagonal slits in order for the heat to penetrate to the interior of the fish.

You can serve it with a simple sauce, melting some butter in a pan and adding salt, pepper, a spoonful of parsley, and some lemon juice.

## Ocean Fish To Roast

Anchovies, eels, squid, cuttlefish, crayfish, grey mullet, dentex, mackerel, haddock, kingfish (only the tail), porgy, sand shark, swordfish, turbot, sardines, sole, tuna, sturgeon, and red mullet.

**FRIED FISH**

*Ingredients for 2 servings:*

**Calculate 3½ oz. per person if the fish is small, a little more if the fish is large
flour, salt, oil**

To make good fried fish doesn't require much but you must observe several basic rules:

a) coat the fish with flour well, shake off the excess;

b) fry the fish in plenty of boiling oil, better if it's olive oil;

c) put the fish on paper towels to absorb the oil;

d) always prepare fried fish at the last minute to avoid having it lie around and turn gooey; this way you won't pine for your mother-in-law's fish!

Excellent fried are: shrimp, octopus, etc.

## STEAMED MACKEREL

*Ingredients for 2 servings:*

**10½ oz. mackerel or eel or haddock**
**7 oz. tomato sauce or peeled tomatoes**
**parsley**
**celery, carrot, onion**
**basil**
**laurel**
**½ glass white wine**
**salt**
**oil**

Clean and wash the fish. Wash and chop the vegetables and herbs.

Put a little oil in a skillet, add the chopped vegetables and herbs, and sauté. Add the fish and brown it.

Add salt and white wine. Let the wine evaporate and add the sliced tomatoes. Cover the pan and cook for 10-15 minutes.

• This is a tasty and economical dish.

✦          ✦          ✦

## SEAFOOD SALAD

*Ingredients for 2 servings:*

**7 oz. mussels**
**3½ oz. shrimp**
**3½ oz. octopus**
**lemon**
**parsley**
**pepper**
**olive oil**
**white wine**
**salt**
**basil, onion, carrot, celery**
**cloves**
**cinnamon**

Put a little water in a pot, add the vegetables, herbs and spices, the white wine, and the salt. Bring to a boil.

When the water boils put in the cleaned and washed octopus and the shrimp. Boil over low heat for 5 minutes. Take the shell off the shrimp and slice the octopus.

In a separate pot, put the mussels (well scrubbed). Cover the pot and steam. The mussels will open with the steam. Let them boil in their own juice for at least 5 minutes.

Put the shrimp, mussels, and octopus in a glass bowl. Season with pepper, chopped parsley, lemon juice, and oil.

• This dish is very healthy, nutritious and tasty. And it'll have your stamp on it!

★        ★        ★

## SOLE IN WHITE WINE

*Ingredients for 6 servings:*

**2  tablespoons butter**
**6  sole**
   **salt**
   **pepper**
   **½ tablespoon flour**
**3½  oz. scallions**
   **½ glass dry white wine**
   **parsley**
   **thyme**
   **laurel**
**7  oz. cream**

Wash and dry the sole and put them in an enamel baking dish that you have greased with butter. Season with salt, pepper, and some chopped scallions.

Sprinkle the melted butter on the fish and add a little white wine to cover them completely. Add a small bunch

of herbs: parsley, thyme, and laurel leaves. Cover with
the cream and put the baking dish in the oven at 475° for
about 20 minutes.

★     ★     ★

## STUFFED WEAKFISH

*Ingredients for 2 servings:*

1  **weakfish, about 10½ oz.**
7  **oz. Russian salad**
1  **glass dry white wine**
2  **oz. mayonnaise**
   **parsley**
   **laurel**
   **basil**
   **celery, carrot, sage, rosemary, cinnamon**
   **cloves**
   **pepper**
   **salt**

Clean and wash the fish. Put 1 quart of water in a pot
together with the wine and all the herbs and spices. Add
the fish and bring to a boil. When it boils, lower the heat
to minimum. Boil for 5 minutes.

Remove the fish from the water and let it cool.

Put the fish on the cutting board and with a sharp
knife cut the fish open along the backbone. Open it carefully and take out the backbone and all bones. Spread the
Russian salad on the fish and decorate with mayonnaise.

Reconstruct the fish and decorate it with mayonnaise
and some parsley sprigs. It's ready.

● This can be an excellent cold dish, a good antipasto, a light and nutritious dish. You can also prepare
whiting, tench, or other fish with delicate meat in this
fashion.

# 7

# VEGETABLES

*Artichokes — Sweet and Sour Onions — Mixed Salad — Artichoke Salad — Spinach Flan — Batter for Fried Vegetables — Fried Potatoes — Potato Pie — Tomatoes — Vegetables Au Gratin — Cauliflower Flan — Asparagus in Pastry — Stuffed Zucchini*

## ARTICHOKES

*Ingredients for 2 servings:*

**4 artichokes**
**1 oz. parsley**
**4 cloves garlic**
**1 glass water**
**1 glass olive oil**
**1 pinch dried fennel seed**
   **or**
**4 sprigs wild fennel (blessed is the one who finds it!)**
   **salt**

Clean the artichokes together with the stalks, which are very good. Cut each artichoke in half and remove the choke.

Put the halved artichokes and their stalks, which have been cut into pieces, in a baking pan.

Add chopped parsley, the peeled garlic cloves, salt, and the fennel plus the oil and water. Put the pan on top of the stove and bring the water and oil to a boil. When it boils, put the pan in the oven.

Bake, uncovered, for 30 minutes in a 400° oven.

● These artichokes are very tasty. They go very well with guinea hen, roasts, and every type of meat and cheese.

## SWEET AND SOUR ONIONS

*Ingredients for 2 servings:*

**14 oz. small flat onions**
**½ glass vinegar**
**1 teaspoon sugar**
**1 tablespoon flour**
**oil**
**salt**

Peel and wash the onions, coat them with flour, and shake off the excess flour.

Put some oil in a pan and brown the onions, then add salt. Add the sugar and vinegar. Cover. Cook over low heat for 15 minutes.

If it dries up too much, add a little cold water.

*Note:* The flour with the addition of the vinegar produces a little sauce that keeps the onions soft and tasty.

Beware of onions sold in plastic bags! They are very convenient because they are already peeled but they have preservatives that alter their wholesomeness. They can be bad for you.

★       ★       ★

## MIXED SALAD (A Convention of Vitamins)

*Ingredients for 2 servings:*

> **carrots**
> **celery**
> **fennel, chicory, radishes**
> **tomatoes, peppers**
> **seasonal salad greens**
> **onions, artichokes**
> 1 **hard-boiled egg**
> **salt, pepper, oil**
> **vinegar**

Clean and wash all the vegetables. Slice them. You can either put all the vegetables together or keep them separated from one another.

Season with salt and pepper that have been mixed in the vinegar or lemon juice. Add the oil.

Grate the egg yolk. Mix.

• Remember for a salad you need: a savant to add salt, a miser to add vinegar, a prodigal to add oil, and a lunatic to toss it!

★      ★      ★

## ARTICHOKE SALAD

*Ingredients for 2 servings:*

> 2 **artichokes**
> 1 **lemon**
>   **oil**
>   **salt**
> 1 **oz. Parmesan cheese**

Clean the artichokes and the stalks (if they are tender) and cut them into quarters.

Take out the choke. Cut into very thin slices along with the stalks. Put the sliced artichokes in a glass bowl, then add salt, lemon juice, and a little oil. Slice the Parmesan. Mix.

- It's excellent!

★ ★ ★

## SPINACH FLAN

*Ingredients for 2 servings:*

1 **bowl white sauce**
2 **eggs**
  **nutmeg**
7 **oz. spinach**
2 **tablespoons crushed bread**
1 **oz. Parmesan cheese**

Prepare the white sauce. When it's cooked, remove from the heat and add 2 pinches of salt and an egg. Stir quickly so the egg doesn't cook.

When the first egg has been absorbed, add the second, stirring quickly. Grate some nutmeg, add the Parmesan, and add the boiled spinach, which has been squeezed and passed through a vegetable grinder. Mix together well.

Butter a rectangular pan ("teflon" or "silverstone" pans do not need to be buttered and work well). Pour the mixture into the selected pan and cook at 400° for 30-40 minutes.

*Remember:*

a) The crushed bread prevents the flan from "dropping" once it's taken out of the oven.

b) Never fill the pan to the top with the mixture because in cooking it expands a lot and you risk it overflowing.

c) If you add only the egg yolks to the white sauce and then add the whipped egg whites, you have the famous soufflés, very soft, but very temperamental. In fact, soufflés "drop" easily. The crushed bread that is added partially helps to prevent this, but there's another secret: after turning off the oven don't take it out right away; leave it in a warm oven for 5-10 minutes.

*Note:* The recipe for spinach flan can also be used to make a flan with artichokes, carrots, zucchini, cauliflower, or onions. In this case the vegetables are cleaned, sliced, and sautéed in butter. Don't make the mistake of blending them: artichokes, zucchini, etc. These vegetables are incorporated into the white sauce (seasoned as above with salt, nutmeg, Parmesan, and eggs), sliced, sautéed in butter, and salted. You can also make a flan with 2 or 3 different vegetables. For example: prepare the seasoned white sauce and divide it into 3 parts: to one part add some carrots sautéed in butter; to another part add the zucchini sautéed in butter; and to the last part, add the boiled spinach. Put the 3 parts in the pan divided but together. You'll get a 3-color flan.

Cheese flan is exceptionally good. Add to the white sauce 7 oz. of cheese (for example, some fontina, some berna, some stacchino, etc.). The rest of the recipe is the same as above.

★          ★          ★

## BATTER FOR FRIED VEGETABLES

*Ingredients for 20 fried pieces:*

**4 oz. flour**
**3 eggs**
   **salt**
**1 teaspoon baking powder**
   **milk, as much as needed**
**1 small glass grappa liqueur**

Put the flour in a bowl. Add the eggs, salt, baking powder, and the grappa. Mix a little and dilute it all with the milk.

You should have a rather liquidy cream. Set it aside for at least 2 hours. Now decide what you want to make!

You can use it to fry: eggplant, zucchini, pumpkin flowers, cauliflower (boiled), Swiss chard (the white part), mushrooms, tomatoes, lemons, oranges, apples, bananas, and cherries.

To make these fried you need to cut them into thin slices, dip them in the batter, and put them in plenty of boiling oil.

★    ★    ★

## FRIED POTATOES

*Ingredients for 6 servings:*

**2½ lbs. potatoes, sliced (about 7 oz. per person)**
 **oil (olive oil is best)**
 **salt**
 **butter**
 **sage**

Put plenty of oil in an iron skillet. When the oil boils put in some of the potatoes that have been washed and dried, not too many. Cook to a golden color without "tormenting" them. They're done when they float on the surface.

Remove the cooked potatoes to paper towels and add salt. Continue in the same way with the rest of the potatoes.

Here's a hint: when the potatoes are done put some butter and sage in a pan and sauté, add the fried potatoes, and put them in the oven for a few minutes.

Besides giving them flavor, this procedure will make the potatoes very tender.

★    ★    ★

## POTATO PIE

*Ingredients for 2 servings:*

10½ oz. boiled potatoes
    nutmeg
 2 tablespoons Parmesan cheese
    milk
 2 tablespoons butter
3½ oz. mozzarella or fontina or sliced American cheese
 2 large slices mortadella
 2 large slices prosciutto
    a round or rectangular pan

If you have boiled or mashed potatoes left over, put them in a pot over minimum heat and add a little milk, making a creamy mixture (like mashed potatoes). Add 2 eggs, nutmeg, and the Parmesan.

Mix vigorously with a wooden spoon. Now grease the pan with butter.

Spread some of the prepared potatoes in the pan. On top of this mixture put the mortadella (which must be sliced thin) or the prosciutto. On top of the mortadella or prosciutto put the chosen cheese, sliced thin.

Cover the mortadella and cheese with the rest of the potato mixture. Spread it well so that the surface is smooth.

Put it in a preheated oven at 475° for about 15-20 minutes. It must not burn, but turn golden. It can be a single course for supper.

You can even prepare it the day before and save it, covered, in the refrigerator.

★      ★      ★

## TOMATOES

*Ingredients for 2 servings:*

**7 oz. tomatoes**
   **salt**
   **oil**
   **vinegar**
   **oregano**

Cut the tomatoes into cubes.

Season them with salt, a pinch of oregano, oil, and vinegar. Mix and taste something good.

★      ★      ★

## VEGETABLES AU GRATIN

*Ingredients for 2 servings:*

**6 oz. of vegetables**
   **butter**
   **Parmesan cheese**
**1 cup white sauce**

Boil the chosen vegetable (artichokes, cardoons, carrots, Swiss chard, cauliflower, etc.).

Cook it in boiling, salted water; it should be tender. Drain, put it in a baking pan, dot with butter, and a little grated Parmesan. Make the white sauce. Pour the white sauce over the vegetable. Bake in the oven at 475° until golden.

It's ready when you see that typical golden crust.

★      ★      ★

## CAULIFLOWER FLAN

*Ingredients for 4 servings:*

10½ oz. cauliflower
1 oz. butter
1 oz. flour
1 oz. grated Parmesan cheese
1 glass milk
2 eggs
  salt, nutmeg

Cook the cauliflower in boiling, salted water, drain and mash it with a fork. Sauté it in butter and add the flour and milk a little at a time; cook for 15 minutes over low heat, stirring constantly. When the mixture is almost cold, add salt, nutmeg, and the 2 eggs, beating for 5 minutes.

Pour the mixture in a greased mold sprinkled with bread crumbs and cook in the top of a double boiler for a good hour.

★      ★      ★

## ASPARAGUS IN PASTRY

*Ingredients for 6 servings (it's a challenging dish and only worth the effort for a certain number of people):*

1 11-inch pie shell not more than 2 inches deep
10½ oz. fondue sauce
3 egg yolks
1 glass milk
10½ oz. asparagus tips
7 oz. thinly sliced prosciutto
3½ oz. Parmesan cheese
2 oz. butter

Buy the pie shell from a good baker. (It's difficult to find it ready-made; I usually order one the day before.)

Cook the asparagus in boiling, salted water. Then remove them from the water.

I use this water from the asparagus to make the fondue sauce. Let me explain: while the asparagus are cooking, I slice some fontina cheese and put it in a copper or aluminum saucepan with a heavy bottom. Then I cover the fontina with the boiling water that the asparagus cooked in. I let the fontina soak for 2 minutes. Then I throw out the boiling water and cover the fontina with milk.

I put the pot over minimum heat and stir constantly with a wooden spoon until the fontina is creamy and melted. Now I remove the pan from the heat and add, one at a time, the 3 egg yolks, stirring constantly. I blend the egg yolks in well, put the pan over minimum heat again, and let the fondue thicken, stirring constantly. Careful! It mustn't boil but only thicken; turn off the heat.

Now I take a baking dish and line it with aluminum foil and put the pie shell in. I put a ladleful of fondue in the pie shell, coating well the interior of the shell. I add a layer of asparagus, which has been dipped in melted butter and then in Parmesan (one even layer—don't pile up layers).

Over this layer of asparagus I put a layer of prosciutto. I put in another ladleful of fondue and another layer of asparagus and prosciutto, ending with the fondue. Now I put my nutritious pie in a preheated oven at 475° for 15-20 minutes.

- Serve hot. It's a chic dish that can be preceded only by "Meat, Alba Style" and followed by a fresh fruit salad.

It can even be prepared a day before and cooled and refrigerated when it's done.

*Note:* Instead of asparagus you can substitute mushrooms, cardoons, or artichokes, thinly sliced and cooked in butter. The rest of the procedure is the same as above.

★      ★      ★

## STUFFED ZUCCHINI

*Ingredients for 2 servings:*

**4 medium-sized fresh zucchini**
***For the stuffing:***
**3½ oz. raw ground meat**
**3½ oz. raw sausage**
**2 eggs**
**2 oz. fresh bread crumbs soaked in milk**
**2 oz. parsley**
  **basil leaves**
  **nutmeg**
**2 tablespoons grated Parmesan cheese**
**2 oz. bread crumbs**

Clean the zucchini, parsley, and basil. Heat to boiling a pot with salted water. When the water boils, add the zucchini and boil for about 10 minutes.

Meanwhile, in a bowl combine the meat, sausage (without the skin), eggs, a little nutmeg and the Parmesan, a little salt, bread crumbs (only 2 tablespoons), chopped parsley, and basil. Mix together. When the zucchini are cooked, cut them in half lengthwise.

Spoon out the insides carefully so as not to break the zucchini. If the zucchini stuffing is tender without large seeds, add it to the mixture in the pot.

Take half a zucchini and fill it with some of the prepared stuffing. Do the same for the rest of the zucchini halves, dividing the stuffing equally.

When the zucchini are all filled, take each one and coat it with bread crumbs; breading it in this way will make it more crispy. Put a sheet of aluminum foil in a baking pan and put the zucchini on the foil. Bake in a 475° oven until golden and they're ready.

● This is an excellent dish. The same stuffing can be used for peppers, tomatoes, eggplants, onions, and potatoes. Peppers, tomatoes, and eggplants are used raw and thus require longer cooking time, but they're great.

# 8

# DESSERTS

*Sicilian Cannoli — Energizing Pineapple — Carnival Sweets — Almond Cream — Classic Pastry Cream — Pastry Cream (Another Version) — Sweet Crepes — Spring Cup — Prince Sweets — Apple Fritters — Fried Squares — Tea Cakes — Party Balls — Fruit Filled Panettone — Jelly Roll — Fresh Fruit Torte — Cream Filled Cake — Apple Cake — Strudel — Hazelnut Sweets*

## SICILIAN CANNOLI

*Ingredients for 25 cannoli:*

**For the dough:**
5¼ oz. flour
1 noce di strutto — lard
1 pinch salt
½ teaspoon sugar
   red or white wine or marsala
   frying oil

**For the cream:**
17 oz. ricotta
 9 oz. powdered sugar
   distilled orange blossom water
   chocolate chips, or candied fruit or pistachio nuts
   vanilla flavored sugar

To make the cannoli you need special tin forms about ¾ of an inch in diameter and about 8 inches long. Cannoli consist of a shell made with a special dough, which is the outside shell, and a ricotta cream inside.

First, prepare the shells. On the table put the flour, lard, a pinch of salt, and the sugar. Mix these ingredients with a little red or white wine or some marsala in order to obtain a rather hard dough. Gather the dough into a ball and set it aside for about 1 hour, covered with a dish cloth.

Then roll out the dough rather thin (1 inch) and cut 12 squares with 4-inch sides. On each square put one of the tin forms, diagonally, and roll the 2 opposite points around the form.

Press these points to seal the cannoli closed. In a skillet with plenty of oil put the tin forms with the dough wrapped around them. The shells are fried to a deep blond color so that they are crispy. It's better to fry one or two at a time, being careful not to break them.

Remove them from the pan and let them cool; then carefully remove the tin forms and let them finish cooling. As the tin forms cool, reuse them to wrap and fry more shells.

When the shells, have been prepared, put the ricotta and powdered sugar in a bowl. Mix, then strain the mixture one or two spoonfuls at a time: you will obtain a very delicate cream that you can flavor with a little orange blossom water.

To this cream you can add some chocolate chips, some candied fruit, or some chopped pistachio nuts, or candied orange peel, whatever you like.

Fill the shells with a spoon or pastry bag. Then using the blade of a knife, even out the cream on the open sides of the shell.

Finally, put a piece of candied fruit in each open end, pushing it into the cream. Place the finished cannoli in a glass dish and sprinkle with vanilla-flavored powdered sugar.

★      ★      ★

## ENERGIZING PINEAPPLE

*Ingredients for 4 servings:*

1 **pineapple, about 2 lbs.**
2 **tablespoons sugar**
1 **small glass of cognac**

Cut the pineapple in slices about ½-inch each.

Cut off the skin, clean the slices, put them in a deep dish, and sprinkle them with sugar and cognac.

They're suitable after a challenging dinner. Prepare them 4 or 5 hours before serving.

● Pineapples are good for you. The sugar and cognac are energizing and they facilitate digestion of the food.

## CARNIVAL SWEETS

*Ingredients for 6 servings:*

8½ **oz. flour**
2 **tablespoons butter**
2 **oz. sugar**
2 **eggs**
½ **glass liqueur**
1 **pinch salt**
9 **oz. frying oil**

Spread the flour on a working surface, then add the melted butter, eggs, salt, sugar and liqueur. Knead well.

When the dough is well-blended, make a ball, wrap it in a dish towel, and put it in the refrigerator for ½ hour. If it turns out too soft, add flour.

Roll out the dough with a rolling pin and cut into strips. With a scalloped wheel cut some strips in assorted shapes (rectangles, squares, etc.).

Heat a skillet with plenty of oil; when it's hot put in the assorted shapes. Brown on both sides. Remove and sprinkle with powdered sugar.

*Note:* The boiling oil will make the sweets light and tasty, not greasy. The liqueur makes them puff up.

The powdered sugar, if put on when they are hot, sticks perfectly to the dough.

- They are typical Carnival treats.

## ALMOND CREAM

*Ingredients for 2 servings:*

**3½ oz. toasted, ground almonds**
   **pastry cream made with 2 egg yolks**

Prepare the pastry cream. Heat some water. When it boils, add the shelled almonds.

Leave them in the water for 3 minutes. Take the skin off (just squeeze them between 2 fingers), put them in a preheated oven at 400°, and toast them. Remove them from the oven and grind them in a coffee grinder.

Add the ground almonds to the pastry cream. Here you have almond cream. Use it for dressing on fruit cocktail. It's excellent served in cups.

- This cream is very good as filling in cakes.

## CLASSIC PASTRY CREAM

*Ingredients for 2 servings:*

**2  egg yolks**
**4  tablespoons sugar**
**4  half shells of milk**
   **lemon rind**

Put the egg yolks in a small copper pot, add the sugar, and beat vigorously with a wooden spoon.

Stir continuously, always in the same direction.

While working with the eggs and sugar, bring the milk to a boil, adding a little rind to the milk. When the milk boils pour it into the pot with the eggs and sugar.

Mix vigorously so that the eggs don't coagulate with the boiling milk. Put the copper pot over minimum heat. Stir constantly until the cream thickens. Careful! It mustn't boil or it will go crazy.

● This cream is the basis for infinite creams. In fact, pastry cream plus some coffee gives you coffee cream. Pastry cream plus lemon juice and lemon rind gives you lemon cream, and so on.

Pastry cream can be served in cups with a pineapple slice and with whipped cream on top. It can be used as cake filling, etc.

★　　　★　　　★

## PASTRY CREAM (Another Version)

*Ingredients for 8 servings:*

**5 egg yolks**
**5 oz. sugar**
**2 oz. flour**
**17½ oz. milk**
　　**piece of lemon rind to boil with the milk and to be**
　　**removed when the cream is ready**

Beat well the 5 egg yolks together with the sugar, then add the flour. Bring the milk to a boil.

Pour the boiling milk into the pot with the whipped eggs. Mix and boil for 2 or 3 minutes.

● This is a cream with a special consistency good for a fresh fruit torte and excellent for cake filling, or to be eaten plain in cups or with fruit cocktail.

**SWEET CREPES**

*Ingredients for 15 servings:*

**4 oz. flour**
**3 eggs**
**1 pinch salt**
**1 cup milk**
**2 tablespoons butter**
**1 tablespoon cognac or rum**
   **sugar**

These constitute the typical preparation for French cuisine.

In a bowl make a well with the flour and put the 3 eggs in the middle with a pinch of salt and a pinch of sugar. Using a wooden spoon, slowly blend the eggs and the flour and add cold milk a little at a time.

When the mixture is smooth and without lumps, add melted butter and a spoonful of cognac or rum.

Take a small pan about 8 inches in diameter, heat it, and, then with a brush dipped in melted butter, lightly grease the bottom of the pan.

Then pour 2 spoonfuls of the prepared mixture into the pan. The amount should be such that in tilting the pan in all directions the mixture will cover the bottom of the pan.

Let the crepe color slightly, shaking the pan occasionally. As soon as the underneath part of the crepe gains a little color, turn it over.

When the other side has cooked, remove it and continue with the rest of the crepes.

Then put the crepes in a large platter, sprinkle them with confectioner's sugar, and serve them hot.

*Here are some other possible combinations for fillings:*

a) apple jelly and crushed amaretto cookies;

b) apple jelly and kirsch;

c) peach jam, cognac (plus almond slivers, if you like);

d) strawberry jam and whiskey.

*Other combinations:*

e) fresh pineapple soaked in maraschino and sugared;

f) candied pineapple; pour kirsch on the crepes and ignite;

g) pieces of glazed chestnuts with rum;

h) strawberries and cream;

i) raspberries and cream;

j) whipped cream with orange extract or grated orange peel (none of the white part, it's very bitter); accompanied by apricot jam diluted with a little water, heated and flavored with a drop of Strega liqueur;

k) to the crepe mixture you can add 1 tablespoon of bitter cocoa and 2 tablespoons of very finely ground coffee and fill the crepes with slightly sweetened whipped cream.

The liqueur used to make the crepes is rum.

The recipe is from Robert Carrier.

★      ★      ★

**SPRING CUP**

*Ingredients for 6 servings:*

3½ oz. butter
1 qt. milk
3½ oz. sugar
3 oz. flour
3½ oz. savoiardi cookies
   red food coloring
   vanilla extract
1 or 2 egg yolks

Bring the milk with the sugar and vanilla to a boil. In a separate pot melt the butter over low heat and as soon as it's melted, add the flour, stirring vigorously. Then pour in the milk (which you have let cool), stirring continuously. When all the warm milk has been added to the butter and flour, bring the mixture to a boil.

Cream #1: take out ⅓ of the cream. Add the egg yolks, one at a time. Heat for a moment. Wet a glass bowl with water and pour in the first cream.

Cream #2: to half of the remaining cream add cocoa (as much as needed) or melted chocolate. Heat for a moment. Dip the savoiardi cookies in the maraschino liqueur, put them in the first cream, and pour the second cream on top.

Cream #3: add a little red food coloring to the last cream to give it a pink color. Put more savoiardi cookies, which have been soaked in liqueur, in the bowl and pour the pink cream on top. The pink cream must be very watery to smooth and cover everything well.

When it's cold, cover or decorate with whipped cream or butter cream.

**PRINCE SWEETS**

*Ingredients:*

1 sponge cake, about 7 oz.
2 oz. evaporated milk
3 oz. baker's chocolate
3 oz. sugar
2 egg yolks
  sweet liqueur, as much as needed
3½ oz. mascarpone cheese (or cream cheese)
5 oz. whipped cream
3½ oz. candied fruit

Prepare the mascarpone cream to fill the sponge cake.

Beat the cream cheese well in a bowl adding a small glass of liqueur. In a separate bowl, blend the egg yolks with the sugar until the sugar is completely absorbed. Then, slowly add the cream cheese, stirring constantly.

Cut the sponge cake in half, soak it well with liqueur, and spread the cream cheese on the cut side. Put the other half of sponge cake on top and soak again with liqueur.

Now prepare the special cream to cover the sponge cake: chop the chocolate and melt it in the top of a double boiler. Slowly add the evaporated milk and you will have a smooth cream. Pour this cream over the sponge cake. Let it cool.

Cut the filled sponge cake into pieces about 1½ inches square. Decorate them with a whipped cream rose and half a candied cherry. Arrange them on a tray in paper cups.

★　　　★　　　★

## APPLE FRITTERS

*Ingredients for 6 servings:*

5 **apples**
 **oil**
 **confectioner's sugar**
 *For the batter:*
4 **oz. flour (1 cup)**
3 **eggs**
1 **teaspoon baking powder**
 **salt**
 **milk, as much as needed to dilute the mixture**
1 **small glass grappa liqueur**

Prepare the batter. Put the flour in a bowl, add the eggs, salt, baking powder, and the grappa, mix a little, and then dilute it with the milk. You should have a rather liquidy cream. Set it aside for at least 15 minutes.

Peel the apples leaving them whole. Core the apples, then wash and dry them. Cut the apples into thin rings, dip the rings in the batter, and fry in plenty of boiling oil. Put the cooked rings on paper towels and sprinkle with confectioner's sugar.

★ ★ ★

## FRIED SQUARES

*Ingredients:*

**2 lbs. bread dough (from the baker)**
**3 oz. raisins**
**2½ oz. candied fruit**
**5 oz. butter**
**4 oz. sugar**
   **oil**
      **confectioner's sugar**

Knead the dough together with the raisins and chopped candied fruit, butter, and sugar.

Blend the ingredients well into the dough, then roll it out about ¼-inch thick. Cut it into 1¼-inch squares.

Let them rise for about 1 hour, then fry them in a pan with plenty of oil. Spread them out on paper towels to absorb the excess oil and sprinkle with confectioner's sugar.

★ ★ ★

## TEA CAKES

*Ingredients for 6 servings:*

**5 oz. flour**
**3½ oz. melted butter**
**4 oz. sugar**
**2 eggs**
**1½ oz. cocoa**

Put all the ingredients, including the butter in a bowl.

Mix with a wooden spoon obtaining a smooth mixture. Grease some molds and fill with the prepared mixture.

If you prefer, you can take out part of the mixture before adding the cocoa—this way you'll have some chocolate and some white. Bake at 400° for about 10 minutes, remove them from the pan, put them on a serving platter, and sprinkle with confectioner's sugar.

With the same mixture you can also make one rectangular cake. In this case bake for 30 minutes.

★    ★    ★

## PARTY BALLS

*Ingredients:*

**3½ oz. mascarpone cheese**
**2 oz. butter**
**3½ oz. confectioner's sugar**
**1 egg yolk**
**2 oz. cocoa**
**4½ oz. dry biscuits**
**1 small glass maraschino liqueur**
  **colored confetti (for decoration)**

In a salad bowl beat together the cheese, butter, confectioner's sugar, and egg yolk.

Beat for 15 minutes, then add the cocoa, maraschino, and crumbled biscuits (put the biscuits in a plastic bag and crush them with a rolling pin until they are just crumbs).

You'll have a very thick mixture. Form small balls and roll them in the tiny confetti.

Keep the balls in the refrigerator before serving: they'll look like bright corianders.

★    ★    ★

## FRUIT FILLED PANETTONE

*Ingredients for 6 servings:*

1 panettone, about 2 lbs.
  zabaglione, made with 2 eggs
10½ oz. whipped cream
10½ oz. fruit in heavy syrup (pineapples, peaches, apricots)
1 glass sweet liqueur
  candied fruit

Cut the base of the panettone (about 1 inch thick).

Empty out the top part of the panettone being careful not to break the crust. Crumble the scooped-out part of the panettone and set it aside in a bowl.

Add the zabaglione, whipped cream, and fruit cut into pieces. Add a little liqueur (maraschino, or rum, or cherry, or créme di café, etc.). With a brush soak the bottom of the panettone and the top shell with liqueur.

Mix the filling (zabaglione is used cold and half is spread on the base of the panettone).

Put the fruit filling in the shell. Put the base on top.

Put it on a serving platter and decorate it with whipped cream and candied fruit.

*Note:* Remember it's best to prepare this filled panettone a day before "destroying" it. This way when you cut it the slices will remain intact. Therefore, decorate just before serving.

# JELLY ROLL

*Ingredients for 6 servings:*

**sponge cake:**

**4 eggs**

**3½ oz. sugar**

**3½ oz. flour**

 *filling:*

**3½ oz. jelly**

 *decoration:*

**11 oz. confectioner's sugar**

**3½ oz. whipped cream**

*Making the sponge cake:* Take an egg and separate it putting the white in one bowl and the yolk in another. To the yolk, add 1 tablespoon of sugar.

Using a wooden spoon, beat the egg yolk and sugar together vigorously (stir always in the same direction, it's important to do this so that the sponge cake will be soft). Add a second yolk and a tablespoon of sugar and continue stirring; add the third and fourth egg yolks, each with one tablespoon of sugar.

Add another tablespoon of sugar (5 tablespoons in all. 1 with each egg plus an extra one).

Continue beating, always stirring in the same direction, until the sugar is completely absorbed and you have a thick cream. Add 5 tablespoons of flour (one at a time) and continue stirring. The resulting mixture will be thick and creamy and difficult to stir. Now whip the 5 egg whites.

Do this: add a good-sized pinch of salt to the egg whites (the salt helps the eggs whites to whip up nicely). Take a whisk and beat the egg whites until they are fluffly like whipped cream. Add them to the egg yolk mixture.

Careful! This is the most delicate and important part. You must blend the mixture very delicately. You'll have problems if you furiously stir it!

The batter is ready when the various ingredients are no longer distinguishable. The batter should be fluffy. This is sponge cake.

If you want to make a cake just grease a pan, then put a tablespoon of sugar and a tablespoon of semolina in the pan letting them coat all the inner surfaces. These facilitate the browning of the sponge cake and also prevent it from sticking to the pan, thereby making it easier to remove. Put the batter in this greased pan and bake it in a hot oven for 30 minutes.

For the first 20 minutes the oven should not be more than 350° and you absolutely cannot open the oven for the first 20 minutes. After 20 minutes you can open the oven to check if the cake has risen and is browned. If it's not brown raise the temperature to 400° baking for another 10 minutes. Turn off the oven and leave the cake in there for at least 10 minutes. This way the cake won't "drop."

In this case we want to have a sheet of sponge cake at least 10 inches wide and 16 inches long, about 1 inch thick.

To obtain this cake you must:

a) take a jelly roll pan;

b) grease it, line it with a sheet of thick wax paper (butcher's paper), and grease the wax paper;

c) spread the batter into the pan on the sheet of wax paper, using a wooden spoon to help spread it to cover the bottom;

d) put the pan in a preheated 400° oven and bake for 10 minutes, but don't let it brown—only the edges should brown;

e) remove the sponge cake from the oven and immediately spread jelly or cream on the surface;

f) roll the sponge cake up lengthwise;

g) cut the roll in two and form a log;

h) cool it, then sprinkle the log with confectioner's sugar, put the whipped cream in a pastry bag, and decorate the log with it.

• Here you have a stupendous dessert!

Don't be frightened, it's more difficult to describe it than to do it!

★ ★ ★

## FRESH FRUIT TORTE

*Ingredients for 8 servings:*

1 **round sponge cake, about 9½ inches in diameter**
**pastry cream made with 6 eggs**
**fruit in season:**
2 **apples, 2 pears, 2 bananas**
7 **oz. strawberries**
7 **oz. blueberries**
7 **oz. raspberries**
2 **peaches, 2 apricots**
  **grapes**
  *Not all the fruit indicated, but what's on hand!*
  *In winter you can use fresh fruit:* **apples, pears,**
    **bananas, tangerines, and oranges plus canned**
    **fruit**
  **sugar and lemons to season the prepared fruit**
1 **jar fruit jelly** *(grape or apricot is best)*

While the pastry cream cools, clean the apples, pears, and bananas. Peel and cut them into thin slices. Oranges and tangerines are peeled and separated into pieces. Peaches and apricots are cut into thin slices. Strawberries, grapes, blueberries, and raspberries are left whole.

It's best to put each fruit in a separate dish. Put some sugar and lemon juice on each type of fruit. With God's bounty thus prepared and the pastry cream tepid, you can begin your masterpiece.

1) Cut the sponge cake into 2 equal layers. Put each one in a round plate (with the cut side on top).

2) Pour half the pastry cream on each sponge cake circle. (As you can see you have 2 cakes — if you only want one . . . save the other half.)

3) Decorate with the selected fruit putting it evenly over the pastry cream. You can begin from the outside with a round of strawberries, then a round of apples, bananas, peaches, and so on until you reach the center where you can put the smallest fruit, blueberries, grapes, etc.

Look in the bakery windows . . . and copy their ideas.

4) Put the jelly in a small saucepan, add 2 tablespoons of water, and put it over minimum heat. With a wooden spoon, stir, making the jelly melt well. Cool it a little, then take a brush, a wide brush, dip the brush in the warm, melted jelly, and delicately brush over the fruit. When the fruit has been covered with the jelly, put the torte in the refrigerator.

• This is an easy cake to make but difficult to write down. It's economical with respect to those sold in bakeries.

It's healthy, nutritious, and pleasing to the eye. The jelly not only is decorative but also serves to prevent the fresh fruit from turning brown. The lemon juice also serves this purpose: it gives flavor, adds vitamins, and prevents the apples, pears, and bananas from turning brown.

You'll have 8 slices of cake you'll never forget.

★ ★ ★

## CREAM FILLED CAKE

*Ingredients for 2 servings:*

1 **fresh sponge cake, 7 oz.**
1 **cup almond cream or pastry cream or zabaglione cream**
1 **tea cup of assorted sweet liqueurs**
7 **oz. pineapple slices or peaches or pears in syrup cherries in syrup or candied**

Cut the sponge cake in half making 2 layers. In a cup put some maraschino, rum, cherry brandy, alkermes, crème di cafe.

Take a brush (one for sweets, not to decorate) and soak the 2 layers of sponge cake. The brush lets you distribute the liqueur better. Spread the almond or other cream over the bottom layer.

Cover with the other layer.

Using the brush, spread the rest of the liqueur over the cake. Decorate the cake with fruit, whipped cream, and candied fruit.

• It looks good, is good, and costs little but is worth much!

★        ★        ★

**APPLE CAKE**

*Ingredients for 6 servings:*

4 oz. sugar
3½ oz. margarine
7 oz. flour
26 oz. apples
   raisins
3 eggs
3 tablespoons milk
1 envelope baking powder
3½ oz. fruit jelly
   salt

Beat the 3 egg yolks with the sugar. Add the melted margarine and the flour with the baking powder (it's better to sift the flour and the baking powder).

Add the milk and beat the mixture until it's fluffy. Add the whipped egg whites. Carefully blend the egg whites into the rest of the mixture. Grease the pan and sprinkle with 2 tablespoons of sugar and 2 tablespoons of semolina.

Pour half the mixture in the pan. Peel the apples and cut into thick slices. Arrange the apple slices on top of the mixture. Sprinkle with raisins. Cover with the remaining mixture. Put in a hot oven (375°). Bake for 45 minutes.

*Note:* 375° may not be right for every oven. Everyone must take into account his or her own oven. 45 minutes is not too much time for an apple cake. Watch the oven.

After 45 minutes remove it from the oven, spread the jelly over the cake, and return it to the oven for 15 minutes. (All sweets with eggs or baking powder are left in the turned-off oven for a little while.)

Remove the cake from the oven and let it cool (to eat it warm would be to desecrate it!).

● It's great for breakfast with tea. Your friends will envy your softness . . . (pardon! that of your dessert).

## STRUDEL

*Ingredients:*

17½ oz. apples
9 oz. flour
3 oz. sugar
3 oz. raisins
1 egg
milk
salt
lemon rind
2 tablespoons butter

Put the flour on a working surface, add the salt, egg, and a little butter.

Mix, adding a little milk to keep the dough soft. Knead well, wrap in a cloth, and set it aside for ½ hour.

Then roll it out very thin and cover part of the dough with sliced, peeled apples. Sprinkle on the raisins, the lemon rind, sugar, and some of the melted butter.

Fold the dough over on itself. Put it in a round greased pan.

Cover the strudel with the rest of the melted butter, sprinkle it with sugar, and bake in a hot oven about 45 minutes.

★     ★     ★

## HAZELNUT SWEETS

*Ingredients for 4 servings:*

4 oz. shelled hazelnuts
1 pinch salt
4 oz. confectioner's sugar
2 egg whites

Whip the egg whites with a pinch of salt, then add the confectioner's sugar and the chopped nuts. Mix well but carefully so as not to ruin the egg whites.

Grease a baking sheet and drop spoonfuls of the mixture on it (tablespoonfuls for large pieces, teaspoonfuls for small pieces). Put it in the oven at 225° and leave them alone until they cool.

- They're very good!

# 9

## SAUCES

*German Fondue — Aurora Sauce — Tomino Cheese Sauce — White Sauce — Olive Sauce — Cream Cheese Sauce with Nuts — Anchovy Sauce — Mayonnaise — Blender Mayonnaise — Easy Tartar Sauce — Green Sauce — Quick Tuna Sauce*

### GERMAN FONDUE

*Ingredients for each serving:*

**3½ oz. fontina cheese**
**1  egg yolk**
    **water, enough to cover the fontina**

If you want a good and quick fondue you must:

a)  cut the fontina into thin slices;

b)  put it in a copper pot or one with a heavy bottom;

c)  cover the cheese with boiling water and leave it like that for 3 minutes;

d)  throw out the water and add enough milk to cover the cheese;

e)  put it over very low heat, stirring constantly with a wooden spoon; when the fontina is melted, remove it from the heat;

f)  add the egg yolks one at a time, mix, return it to the heat, and stir until creamy.

If it doesn't come out right, take it off the heat and add a teaspoon of dried potato flakes plus another egg yolk.

Return to the heat and continue stirring until the mixture thickens.

Serve it plain or with a thinly sliced truffle, or use it to season potato gnocchi, boiled potatoes, etc., and boiled rice.

✶     ✶     ✶

## AURORA SAUCE

*Ingredients for 2 servings:*

**1 cup mayonnaise**
**2 tablespoons catsup**
**1 teaspoon coffee brandy**

Put the mayonnaise in a bowl, then add the catsup and brandy. Mix and it's ready.

• It's excellent for boiled fish, shrimp cocktail, and frankfurter salad.

★     ★     ★

## TOMINO CHEESE SAUCE

*Ingredients for 2 servings:*

**2 fresh tomino cheeses**
**3½ oz. oil**
  **the juice of 1 lemon**
**1 pinch salt**
**1 pinch pepper**

Put the cheese in a bowl. With a wooden spoon, mash and mix it. Add the salt and pepper. Add the oil, a little at a time, stirring continuously, as you do when making mayonnaise. When all the oil has been added, add the lemon juice. It's ready.

• This sauce is excellent over boiled asparagus, spread on toast, with boiled vegetables in general, or even eaten with bread. Spread it on bread for picnics or a cold supper.

★     ★     ★

## WHITE SAUCE

This recipe is short, sure, and quick—and it's our own!

*Ingredients for a bowl of white sauce:*

**2 oz. butter**
**2 oz. flour**
**17½ oz. milk**
   **salt**

Melt the butter in a copper or steel pot with a heavy bottom; pour in the flour all at once.

Mix well to smooth out the lumps. Add warm or hot milk *a little at a time*. Mix, add salt, and cook for at least 10 minutes.

*Note:* If you want the white sauce for baked lasagna or vegetables au gratin, the white sauce should be thin. If you need it for flan or croquettes, it should be thick.

★    ★    ★

## OLIVE SAUCE

*Ingredients for 2 servings:*

**3½ oz. robiola del bec cheese (mascarpone cheese**
   **can be substituted)**
**2 tablespoons olive cream**

Put the cheese in a bowl, mix vigorously with a wooden spoon, and add the olive cream. It's ready.

• This sauce is excellent spread on bread. You can stuff tomatoes with it. It's nutritious and easy to digest.

*Note:* Olive cream is found in the deli. It's very expensive. Make your own like this: 3½ oz. of black or green olives and 2 oz. of butter.

Remove the pits from the olives, put the olives and butter in the blender, and blend together.

• It's ready, costs little, and has no preservatives.

## CREAM CHEESE SAUCE WITH NUTS

*Ingredients for 2 servings:*

**3½ oz. walnuts (in their shells)**
**1 small package cream cheese**

Shell the nuts and grind them. Put the cream cheese in a bowl and mix with a wooden spoon. When it's creamy, add the ground nuts.

It's ready.

• This sauce is excellent spread on fresh bread or better yet on whole wheat bread. You can also make little balls.

In making balls it's best to reserve some of the ground nuts so that the balls can be coated with them.

It's excellent as an antipasto or a cold dish. (If you can't find cream cheese, mascarpone can be substituted: it's nutritious and a little heavier, but equally as good.)

## ANCHOVY SAUCE

*Ingredients for 2 servings:*

**2 oz. butter**
**2 tablespoons anchovy paste**

Slice the butter and put it in a bowl. Mix vigorously with a wooden spoon.

When the butter is creamy, add the anchovy paste and mix together well. It's ready.

● This sauce is excellent spread on whole wheat bread and can be used as a cold course. It's great as a snack if offered with an aperitif.

I spread it on bread and then I put a slice of smoked salmon on top, or a slice of speck, or in an emergency 2 slices of mortadella.

If I want to be elegant I put the anchovy sauce in a pastry bag and fill small tarts or form little puffs on a plate for antipasto. In this way I obtain a dish more in demand and very effective. In this case it's best if the mixture is cold so that the designs will hold their shape.

★　　★　　★

## MAYONNAISE

*Ingredients for 2 servings:*

**3½ oz. olive oil**
**1　egg yolk**
**lemon juice**
**salt**
**pepper**

This is not difficult. But before beginning, remember these little tips:

1) Never use oil or eggs which have been refrigerated, because the mayonnaise won't hold. All the ingredients must be at room temperature.

2) Use a warm container, put the salt in the egg yolk, and stir for a few seconds before adding the oil.

3) Pour the oil in the beginning drop by drop, always stirring in the same direction.

4) Stir evenly, not in spurts. In fact, very nervous people will never succeed in making mayonnaise.

Put the egg yolk in a bowl, add a pinch of salt and a pinch of pepper, mix, and add the oil a little at a time.

Add the lemon juice a little at a time. If you want thick mayonnaise, add little lemon juice.

If you want it thin, add it without worry.

If the mayonnaise goes crazy you can remedy it by slowly (as if it's oil) pouring it in another warm, wet bowl. Or sometimes all that's needed is to put it in the refrigerator for a few minutes and then stir it again.

★     ★     ★

## BLENDER MAYONNAISE

This sauce takes only a few minutes to make. Put the egg yolk, salt, pepper, lemon juice, and a little oil in the blender. Blend for a few seconds and add the rest of the oil a little at a time.

● This mayonnaise is good but "anonymous." It's certainly not that of your mother-in-law! Mayonnaise is used to dress salads, for boiled meats, to stuff tomatoes, to decorate dishes, etc.

★     ★     ★

## EASY TARTAR SAUCE

*Ingredients for 2 servings:*

1 cup mayonnaise
1 tablespoon capers in vinegar
½ tablespoon chopped parsley
1 oz. pickles
1 hard-boiled egg
3 tablespoons oil

Prepare the mayonnaise, then finely chop the capers, parsley, and pickles. Shell the egg and dice it.

Mix the chopped ingredients with the mayonnaise, then delicately add the diced egg. Finally, very delicately add the oil so that a velvet-smooth sauce results.

• Use for: fried or grilled fish, hard-boiled eggs, cold meat or raw ground meat.

★    ★    ★

## GREEN SAUCE

*Ingredients for 2 servings:*

1 **handful parsley leaves**
1 **clove garlic**
2 **anchovy fillets or 2 teaspoons anchovy paste**
1 **slice bread soaked in vinegar**
2 **tablespoons wine vinegar**
4 **tablespoons olive oil**

Wash the parsley, peel the garlic, and remove the bones from the anchovies.

Soak the bread in the vinegar.

Put the parsley, garlic, anchovies, and the soaked bread on a cutting board. Finely chop everything. Put the chopped mixture in a bowl, add the vinegar and oil, and blend all together.

It's ready.

• Use it on boiled veal and boiled tongue, to stuff tomatoes, on hard-boiled eggs cut in half, tomino cheese, sandwiches, boiled beans, boiled potatoes, boiled string beans, etc.

*Note:* If you want to make this sauce in a few minutes, just put all the ingredients in the blender. It's ready.

But if you want a "green" sauce like your mother-in-law's you must chop all the ingredients with a chopping knife. It will be better because it's not abused by the blades and the heat of the blender's motor.

If you like you can add to the ingredients above: some capers, a hard-boiled egg yolk, green pepper, a hot pepper, cucumber, and plum tomatoes.

But the classic sauce is the one that I have presented above.

★     ★     ★

## QUICK TUNA SAUCE

*Ingredients for 1 cup:*

1  **cup mayonnaise**
1  **oz. tuna**
1  **tablespoon capers**
2  **salted anchovies (without bones and washed)**
    **or**
1  **teaspoon anchovy paste**
2  **tablespoons wine vinegar**

Put all the ingredients in a blender and blend until a smooth mixture results.

● Use it on boiled meat, beef bourguignonne, sandwiches, hard-boiled eggs, boiled potatoes, boiled beans, etc.

*Note:* If you don't have a blender, put all the ingredients through a vegetable grinder and then add the mayonnaise.

# 10

# HOMEMADE LIQUEURS, BEVERAGES, AND SHERBERTS

*Arquebuse Liqueur — Genepi Liqueur — Elder Blossom Drink — Cherries in Alcohol — Lemon Liqueur — Herb Liqueur — Mint Liqueur — Fruit Sherbert*

## ARQUEBUSE LIQUEUR

*Ingredients for 1 bottle of liqueur:*

3 arquebuse leaves
10½ oz. alcohol
9 oz. sugar
14 oz. water

Put the 3 leaves of arquebuse in 10½ oz. of 90 proof alcohol. Leave it for 3 days.

Prepare the syrup: 14 oz. of water plus 9 oz. of sugar, boil for 3 minutes, then cool. To the cooled syrup add the alcohol without the leaves (to filter the alcohol I simply use a strainer covered with sterile gauze; if you want it very pure, filter it with the appropriate filter, which you can find in stores selling equipment for wine making). Bottle it. It's ready immediately but is better after 3 months.

★ ★ ★

## GENEPI LIQUEUR

*Ingredients for a quart:*

1 qt. alcohol for liqueur
40-60 genepi plants
1 qt. water
14 oz. sugar

276

Put the cleaned plants in the alcohol. Leave them like this for at least 45 days. Shake occasionally.

At the end of this time take one qt. of water and bring it to a boil. Now, turn off the heat, pour in 14 oz. of sugar and mix until the sugar is well melted.

While the sugared water is cooling, filter the alcohol, squeezing the plants, which are then discarded.

When the water is cold, mix it with the filtered alcohol. Filter again. With time it will cloud up again; it must be filtered from time to time (3-5 months, if there's any left!).

*Genepi* made like this is about 45 proof. If you want it less strong (and perhaps sweeter), you need to increase the water a little as well as the sugar.

★    ★    ★

## ELDER BLOSSOM DRINK

*Ingredients:*

5 qts. water
5 elder blossoms, just bloomed
3 glasses sugar
1 glass vinegar
1 sliced lemon

Combine all the ingredients, leave for 3 days, and then filter. Drink cold.

★    ★    ★

## CHERRIES IN ALCOHOL

*Ingredients for 2 pounds of cherries:*

¾ **pure alcohol**
¼ **cherry brandy**
**2 oz. sugar**
**2 cloves**

Take the cherries (choose ripe, whole ones), cut the stems close to the fruit, and clean them with a cloth without washing them. Put them in a glass jar, cover with the liqueur indicated above and the cloves. Close the jar and keep in a cool place.

★    ★    ★

## LEMON LIQUEUR

*Ingredients:*

½ **qt. alcohol for liqueurs**
**the very thin skin of 4 medium-sized lemons (only the yellow part)**
**14 oz. sugar**
½ **qt. water**

Let the lemon rind macerate in the alcohol for 20 days.

After this time has passed, strain and add the cooled syrup. Let it age for some time if you want to enjoy it.

● It's excellent cold.

*Syrup:* boil the water, add the sugar, stir with a wooden spoon (or whatever you prefer) until the sugar is melted, let it cool, add it to the alcohol essence, and filter with a paper filter.

The same procedure is used for orange or tangerine liqueur, but in the latter case you must notably increase the number of tangerines.

**HERB LIQUEUR**

*Ingredients:*

    5  laurel leaves
    5  sprigs rosemary
    5  mint leaves
    5  basil leaves
    5  lemon leaves
    1  pinch nutmeg
    ½ qt. pure alcohol
    ½ qt. water
    14 oz. sugar

Put the laurel, rosemary, mint, basil, lemon leaves, and nutmeg in a hermetically sealed jar with the alcohol and leave it for 20 days. Then strain it, make the syrup, and when it's cold add it to the essence. Filter it, bottle it and . . . forget about it.

● It will be excellent when you rediscover it.

**MINT LIQUEUR**

*Ingredients:*

    60 mint leaves
    1  qt. alcohol
    1  qt. water

Put the mint leaves in the alcohol and leave them for a week. On the 7th day boil the water with the sugar.

Boil for 3 minutes, then cool the syrup. Strain the alcohol and add it to the cold syrup. Bottle it. It's ready immediately, but it's better after 3 months.

● It aids digestion, quenches thirst, and tastes good!

If you substitute the same amount of sage leaves for the mint, you will obtain a formidable liqueur that aids digestion and works as a laxative.

## FRUIT SHERBERT

*Ingredients:*

**17½ oz. pureed fruit**
**10½ oz. sugar**
 **1  glass water**

Make the syrup. When it cools add the chosen fruit.
Put it in the freezer. Stir occasionally.

# 11

## HOMEMADE PRESERVES

*FRUIT: Apricots in Syrup — Apricots in Marsala — Dried Apricots — Apricot Marmalade — Morello Cherries in Alcohol — Morello Cherry Jam — Cherries in Syrup — Cherries in Alcohol — Quince Jam — Quince Jam with Brandy — Convent Figs — Dried Figs in Liqueur — Fig Preserves — Fig Jam with Brandy — Strawberries in Syrup — Strawberry Jam — Fruit in Syrup*

*VEGETABLES: Peeled Tomatoes — Raw Tomato Sauce — Roasted, Stuffed Peppers — Antipasto, Piedmont Style*

## Preserving Fruit: General Rules

### Calendar of Fruit Preserving:

*January:* oranges, pineapples, grapefruit, bananas
*February:* oranges, pineapples, lemons, grapefruit
*March:* oranges, pineapples, lemons, grapefruit
*April:* oranges, grapefruit, lemons
*May:* strawberries, rhubarb
*June:* cherries, Morello cherries, plums, apricots
*July:* apricots, Morello cherries, melons, plums, currants, raspberries
*August:* grapes, peaches, melons, plums, blueberries, currants, cornel berries, raspberries
*September:* figs, blueberries, mulberries, plums, grapes
*October:* chestnuts, apples, prickly pears, grapes
*November:* quinces, chestnuts, prickly pears, pears, apples
*December:* tangerines, pears, apples, bananas

## Picking, Gathering, and Cleaning the Fruit

The morning, after the sun has dried the nighttime dew, is the ideal moment to pick fruit for preserving. The fruit should be chosen from among the best, ripe, whole, and, if possible, not treated with chemicals or preservatives and picked at the height of the season. Therefore, it's not advisable, besides being wasteful, to preserve the first fruits because they are perishable.

If you buy the fruit at the market rather than pick it yourself, you must select it with care, following the qualifications stated above. Naturally, in the second case, you can't be sure that the fruit wasn't chemically treated; so clean it carefully before you proceed to preserve it.

In any case it should be washed quickly because fruit loses vitamins and aroma in water. Knowing this, the best thing you could do is to clean the fruit by rubbing it with a clean, damp cloth. If pits must be removed from the fruit, it should be washed first.

While picking keep in mind the way the fruit will be used; for example, if you want to make marmalade, jelly, or preserves the fruit can be without stems, but if you intend to preserve it in alcohol or acquavite (like cherries, grapes, etc.) the fruit should be cut with a little piece of the stem. If possible, the operations for preserving the fruit should be done during the day. The fruit should be kept in a dry, well-aired place to avoid its spoiling.

## Preserving While Hot

As regards marmalade, preserves, and jelly, it's advisable to fill the jars hot. Proceed like this: scald the first jar before pouring in the marmalade. As soon as the marmalade is removed from the heat pour it into the jars, filling them to within ½ inch from the top. Quickly close and hermetically seal the jars and put them in a place where there are no drafts (they must not be submitted to jumps in temperature).

You can wrap the jars in a cloth, leaving them until they are completely cooled. Then keep them in the pantry, in the dark or at least out of direct light. With this method it is also possible to preserve marmalade that is not very thick, that is, with less sugar for those who prefer their foods less sweet.

## Preserves in Alcohol

To preserve fruit in alcohol it's advisable to use a good grade alcohol since the juice from the fruit mixed with the alcohol lowers its gradation.

By the process of osmosis you will have an equal amount of water in the fruit as in the alcohol in which it's preserved.

About one month after jarring the fruit in the alcohol, you must add, for every 2 lbs. of fruit (therefore, weigh it before putting it in the jars), a syrup made with 9 oz. of sugar melted with one tablespoon of water; boil for 1 or 2 minutes and cool.

## Sterilization, Environment for Preserving

When the product to preserve and sterilize is ready and the jars also are washed and dried, you can proceed to jar the product. When the jar is filled, carefully clean the rim, take the rubber seals out of the cold water letting them drip, then put them on the jars, put the cover on, and seal. The jar is ready to be sterilized.

As a general rule you must remember this: the jars with hot contents must be immersed in warm water, or water the same temperature as the jars. Jars with cold contents are put into cold water. Sterilization kills microorganisms that can damage the preserved food and creates an environment unfavorable to the development of microorganisms.

Sterilization occurs through heat and more accurately, by boiling. There are appropriate receptacles on the market for this purpose (but you can use normal pots, too) at reasonable prices. Sterilization neither changes nor alters the organic properties of food. Rather, it preserves the essential characteristics of it.

The receptacle used for sterilization, whatever it is, must have rather high sides and be at least 4 inches higher than the jars to be sterilized so that the water will cover the jars by at least 1 inch above their covers. It's also better if the receptacle is rather wide in order to accommodate more jars at a time. Putting it on top of the stove you can turn on more than one gas jet at the same time to heat the water more rapidly. Put some newspaper on the bottom of the receptacle so that the jars don't break while boiling.

During sterilization, when the water is boiling, the jars should not come into contact with one another, but should be separated from one another by a piece of thin cardboard inserted vertically. If the water evaporates before sterilization is completed, you must add more boiling water so as not to stop the boiling process.

Sterilization time must be calculated from the moment the water begins to boil till the instant you turn off the heat with a 5-minute leeway. The sterilized jars must then remain in the water until it has completely cooled.

Check the jars to see that the sterilization process is perfect. You do this by unhooking the steel lever that keeps the cover tight on the jars: if the unhooked cover remains perfectly sealed on the jar, even when you try to lift the cover, the sterilization is perfect. If this is not the case you need to repeat the operation, checking, however, the condition of the rubber and the sealing of the cover, because there may be some defect.

The sterilized jars are then put in a dry and dark place. During the first week check them each day. If in some jars you see signs of change (bubbles, muddiness, etc.), open each one and use it immediately, cooking the product, naturally, smelling it and looking at it: if it smells bad, throw it out without hesitation.

When the jars have been put away, avoid, as much as possible, frequently changing the location and environment because the change in temperature, the dryness or humidity in the air, can alter the elasticity of the rubber seals on the jars. The ideal place would be a dry wine cellar.

To open the sterilized jars, just unhook the lever and pull the rubber toward you. If a jar is difficult to open just put the cover under hot water, then pull the rubber or unscrew it if the cover is the screw type.

Once the product has been opened it's advisable to eat it within a short time, keeping it in the refrigerator.

Just before placing the jars or bottles in the pantry, put a label on each one with the contents, date of preparation, ingredients, the period of waiting time before consuming the product, and the time by which it should be consumed. Besides this you should leave space for critical notes or variations that will be useful when opening the jar.

## APRICOTS IN SYRUP

*Ingredients:*

**6½ - 7½ lbs. whole apricots, not too ripe**
**12 - 14 oz. sugar**
 **1 piece of lemon rind**
 **1 qt. water**

Quickly wash the apricots in cold water, then dry them with a clean cloth, placing them in the sun for a half hour. Meanwhile, prepare the syrup: mix the sugar and lemon rind together with the water and boil for 2-3 minutes, then cool the syrup.

Divide the apricots in half with the aid of a sharp knife and discarding the pit, place them in the jars with the cut side toward the bottom, pushing and arranging them so as to fit as many as possible in the jar.

When the syrup has cooled, pour it over the apricots filling up to an inch above the top layer of fruit.

Seal the jars and sterilize them for 15-20 minutes. Keep them in a dark, dry place, checking that they are perfectly sealed.

For the first 10 days check that the jars are perfectly sterilized and closed.

Eat immediately those apricots whose syrup begins to cloud up.

★          ★          ★

## APRICOTS IN MARSALA

The syrup from the apricots becomes a delicious drink.

*Ingredients:*

**6½ lbs. whole apricots, not overripe**
**21 oz. sugar**
**14 oz. water**
**½ qt. dry marsala**
**1 lemon**
**2 cloves**
**1 pinch cinnamon**

First boil the water with the sugar for a moment until the sugar melts.

Remove the syrup from the heat and add the marsala, a piece of lemon rind and lemon juice, the cinnamon and cloves. Let it cool.

Meanwhile, carefully clean the apricots or quickly wash them in cold water and air dry.

Cut them in half with a sharp knife and remove the pit, then gather them together in the jars.

When the apricots are all placed in the jars and the marsala is cold, pour it over the apricots covering them to ¾ of their height. The liquid should remain at least ½ inch below the rim of the jar.

Hermetically seal the jars and sterilize them for 10 minutes. Store them in a cool, dark place.

★   ★   ★

## DRIED APRICOTS

*Ingredients:*

**ripe apricots**

Cut the apricots in half and remove the pits. Arrange them on grills that can be put in the oven, not too hot.

Put them in the oven for a few hours and then leave them there for a couple of days afterward. When they have all shriveled up, expose them to the open air for 3 or 4 days, in the sun, discarding those that are spoiled. It is necessary to check that evaporation proceeds as quickly as possible, without, however, the fruit drying up. For the time when they are in the open air (covered with a cloth or waxed paper) remember to take them in at night, so that the humid night air will not soften them again. Then place them in very clean wooden boxes.

Generally, before using the apricots in desserts, it will be necessary to soak them for a half hour in water or liqueur to facilitate their cooking.

## APRICOT MARMALADE

*Ingredients:*

**9 lbs. apricots**
**4 lbs. sugar**
**1 lemon**

Quickly wash the apricots of any chemical residue, then drain and remove the pits.

Cut half the apricots into small pieces and put them in the cooking pot. The other half, mash and pass through a sieve. Add these to the apricots already in the pot and add the lemon juice and a pinch of grated lemon rind. Put the pot on the heat and let it boil, slowly, skimming the foam, for a couple of minutes. Then add the sugar and return to a boil, letting it cook and slowly thicken, stirring frequently.

When the marmalade reaches the correct consistency, remove it from the heat and immediately pour it in the jars and seal them.

Store in the pantry.

★　　　★　　　★

## MORELLO CHERRIES IN ALCOHOL

"Morello cherries in Alcohol," besides being an excellent digestive, can be used to decorate desserts, ice cream, and puddings.

*Ingredients:*

**2 lbs. ripe sour cherries**
**7 oz. sugar**
   **alcohol for desserts**
**1 cinnamon stick**
   **some cloves**
   **some bitter almonds**

Cut the stem of the cherries about 1 inch from the fruit, wash them quickly, or simply rub them with a clean cloth, delicately dry them, and let them finish air-drying.

Put the cherries into absolutely clean, dry jars with lids that seal hermetically. Add the sugar, cinnamon, cloves, almonds, and enough alcohol to cover the cherries.

Seal the jars and keep in the pantry or a dry, dark place.

I suggest waiting at least 3 months before tasting the cherries so that they can slowly absorb the alcohol and lend their taste to the preserving liquid.

★　　　★　　　★

## MORELLO CHERRY JAM

*Ingredients:*

6½ lbs. ripe Morello cherries, already pitted
3 lbs. 5 oz. sugar
1 lemon
1 small glass maraschino
½ glass water

As soon as the cherries have been washed and pitted gather them together in a bowl, squeezing the lemon juice over them and adding the grated lemon rind (naturally without the white part underneath because it's bitter).

Heat a large pot (large enough to hold the cherries) with the sugar and let it boil adding the water. As soon as the sugar has melted and begins to boil, pour in the cherries. Mix and continue boiling, slowly, skimming the foam and stirring constantly with a wooden spoon.

When the sugar becomes thick and glue-like, that is, when the jam has thickened to its normal density (several drops of jam poured on an inclined plate will drip very slowly), remove the pot from the heat, adding the maraschino. Mix and pour into the jars hot, sealing them.

Store in a cool, dark place.

★　　　★　　　★

## CHERRIES IN SYRUP

*Ingredients:*

**6½ lbs. whole, ripe cherries**
**14-17½ oz. sugar**
**1 qt. water**
**a few drops maraschino extract (optional)**

Put the cherries in cold water and wash them. Then drain them, handling them carefully so as not to mar them. Remove the stem.

Spread them out to dry, then gather them together and fill the jars.

Prepare the syrup: bring the water and sugar and a piece of lemon rind to a boil. Let the syrup boil for 3-4 minutes and let it cool.

When the syrup is cool, pour it over the jarred cherries filling a little more than ¾ of the way. If you want more of a cherry aroma add some maraschino extract to each jar.

Seal the jars and sterilize them for 20-30 minutes.

Store in a cool, dark place. You can substitute cherry brandy for the maraschino.

## CHERRIES IN ALCOHOL

*Ingredients:*

**2 lbs. whole cherries**
**14 oz. sugar**
**½ glass water**
   **grappa or other liqueur that you like**
   **some cherry leaves**

Wash and dry the cherries with a dishcloth, cutting the stem close to the fruit, about ½ inch from the base. Then let them air-dry completely.

Put the perfectly clean and dried cherries in jars with hermetically sealing lids.

Prepare the syrup: melt the sugar with ½ glass of water, boiling for about 3 minutes. Then cool it and pour it over the cherries, completing the filling process with grappa or other liqueur of your choice.

To each jar add a piece of lemon rind and cherry leaves. Seal the jar and store in the pantry.

I advise waiting at least 3 months before tasting the cherries so that they can absorb the alcohol.

The addition of a few bitter almonds will serve to perfume the liquid.

★          ★          ★

## QUINCE JAM

*Ingredients:*

**2 lbs. 6 oz. quinces**
**3 lbs. sugar**
**the juice of 2 lemons and a piece of lemon rind**
**½ glass water**

Peel and core the quinces. Put them in a container with cold water and the juice of one and a half lemons to prevent their turning brown.

Drain and put them in a pot with ½ glass of water, the rest of the lemon juice, and the lemon rind. Bring to a slow boil and stir, then continue cooking.

When the quinces are cooked, mash and pass them through a stainless steel sieve.

Return them to the pot, add 2 lbs. of sugar, and bring to a boil, stirring and skimming off the foam, until it reaches the consistency of marmalade and is smooth.

While the quince jam is still hot, put it into molds to give it the chosen shape, or spread it on a surface sprinkled with sugar, keeping the thickness to ½ inch.

When it's cold cut it as you wish.

Dip it in the sugar and store it in closed, dry containers.

★ ★ ★

## QUINCE JAM WITH BRANDY

*Ingredients:*

**3 ripe quinces**
**2 lbs. sugar**
**3 lemons**
**1 small glass brandy**

Remove the stem and any bruises and wash the quinces in cold water. Cut them into pieces discarding the seeds also, then put them in a pot adding some lemon rind and lemon juice and covering them with water. Boil slowly, stir occasionally, and skim the foam.

If the water evaporates before the quinces are cooked, add more boiling water.

When they are cooked, drain them; then while they're hot pass them through a sieve gathering the puree to weigh it.

To the puree (it should be about 2 pounds), add 2 pounds of sugar.

Return to heat, letting it cook slowly and stirring until it reaches its maximum density.

It is necessary to stir constantly over very low heat. Before taking the quince jam from the heat (it should be reduced to about 2 pounds) add a little glass of brandy. When it's as thick as polenta, take it off the heat.

Prepare a suitable plate or slab on which to put the quince jam and sprinkle it with a little of the remaining sugar. Pour the jam in the plate and spread it to about ½-inch thick. Sprinkle some more sugar on top and put the plate in a cool and aired place to cool the jam.

When it's cold and hard, cut it into the shapes desired.

Roll the pieces in sugar and store them in a milk container, in an absolutely dry place.

★ ★ ★

## CONVENT FIGS

*Ingredients:*

6½ lbs. ripe, firm figs
3 lbs. sugar
10½ oz. walnuts (shelled)
2 lemons
3 shot glasses brandy
a little water

Carefully and quickly wash the figs, put them on a cloth, and let them dry in the sun for an hour.

Cut the figs in half, then put a quarter of a walnut inside each half fig and close it. Put the half figs directly into a jar, layering them. Over each layer sprinkle a handful of sugar (the sugar must be enough for all the figs), a piece of lemon rind, a few drops of lemon juice, and a shot glass of brandy.

When the jar is full (the final layer of figs must be at least ½ inch below the rim), add a few spoonfuls of boiling water over the figs to have a little syrup when you eat the figs. Seal the jar and sterilize for 45 minutes.

Store in a dark, dry place.

★  ★  ★

## DRIED FIGS IN LIQUEUR

*Ingredients:*

**dried figs
sugar
shelled walnuts, cut into quarters
liqueur (grappa or rum)**

For this recipe you can use store-bought dried figs or those which you have dried in the sun, after having hung them on a string by their stems in the open air and sunshine. Cut the figs in half and in each half put a quarter of a walnut. Then, if possible, try to enclose it in the middle of the fig.

Put the figs in a jar, close together with the nut facing the bottom. Over each layer of figs sprinkle a spoonful of sugar and a shot glass of liqueur.

Close the jars and wait a few days for the figs to slowly absorb the liqueur. Reopen the jars and add enough liqueur to cover the figs. Close the jars and store in a dry place.

★  ★  ★

## FIG PRESERVES

*Ingredients:*

2 lbs. figs, whole and not overripe
14 oz. sugar
2 lemons
1 teaspoon grated lemon rind
   cinnamon (optional)
   liqueur (optional)

Use a plastic grater to grate the lemon rind avoiding the white part of the skin, which is bitter.

Peel the figs and layer them in a large pan, alternating each layer with sugar, lemon juice, and grated lemon peel. Cover and set aside for a couple of hours.

Put it over the heat and let it simmer for 1 hour carefully, frequently stirring with a wooden spoon. Set it aside for 12 hours and then boil again for 1 hour.

Let it cool and put the jam into jars and sterilize for 10 minutes. Store in a cool place.

If you like you can also flavor the jam with some cinnamon or liqueur.

★      ★      ★

## FIG JAM WITH BRANDY

*Ingredients:*

5½ lbs. ripe figs
2 lbs. sugar
½ lemon or a piece of lemon rind
1 shot glass of brandy

Remove the stems and the skin. Then cut them into pieces and put them in a large pot (not aluminum) and set them aside for 1 hour. Add the sugar and the lemon rind and boil, slowly, stirring continuously with a wooden spoon and skimming the foam.

When the jam reaches the desired thickness, mix in the small glass of brandy and the lemon juice. Finish cooking, being careful that the jam doesn't stick to the bottom of the pan.

Pour it into jars while it is still hot and seal hermetically.

Store in a cool, dry place.

## STRAWBERRIES IN SYRUP

The strawberries can be used for cake fillings and pies, also to garnish fruit salads and various desserts.

*Ingredients:*

> 4½ lbs. strawberries, not overripe, about the same size
> 17½ oz. sugar
> 1 qt. water
> some lemon peel
> a little brandy or alcohol for liqueur

It's not advisable to wash the strawberries, but if it's necessary wash them quickly in a way that doesn't soak them with water. Then spread them on a cloth to dry in the sun for an hour.

Put the strawberries, very dry, into small jars. Prepare the syrup mixing the water with the sugar and letting it boil 3-5 minutes. Pour the boiling syrup over the strawberries in the jars. Fill to ¾ full. Put a piece of lemon peel in each jar.

Since strawberries are a very delicate fruit and a long sterilization can damage them, it is advisable to pour a few drops of heated brandy into the cover of the jar (the part which is inside once the jar is closed). Ignite the brandy and while the alcohol is burning slowly close the jar.

The alcohol will consume the oxygen inside the jar. Then sterilize the jars for about 5 minutes, checking afterward to see that the covers are well-sealed.

Store the strawberries in a dry, dark place.

★        ★        ★

## STRAWBERRY JAM

*Ingredients:*

**6½ lbs. strawberries**
**3¾ lbs. sugar**
**1 lemon**
**1 shot glass maraschino liqueur**
**1 glass water**

Choose perfectly ripe strawberries without bruises. If they are really dirty you need to wash them rapidly.

Put the dried strawberries in a bowl. Squeeze the lemon juice over them and also add the grated lemon peel. Boil the sugar with the glass of water being careful that the sugar doesn't brown.

When the sugar is melted, let it boil for 3-4 minutes. Remove from the heat and pour it over the strawberries in the bowl while it is still hot. Mix the strawberries and the syrup in a pot and let them boil, slowly, stirring.

When the jam has thickened to the proper consistency, add the maraschino and immediately pour it, hot, into jars, hermetically sealing them. Store them in a cool, dark, place.

## FRUIT IN SYRUP

*Ingredients:*

**peaches, pears, apricots, cherries, plums, mulberries, raspberries, figs**

A very simple procedure: peel peaches and pears, cut them into pieces, without washing them, and put them into glass jars that seal hermetically.

When you have filled the jars with the selected fruit, add only 3 tablespoons of sugar, seal the jars, and put them in cold water. Bring to a boil and boil for 20 minutes.

After cleaning apricots, plums, and cherries with a damp dish towel, put them in glass jars with hermetically sealing lids. Add 3 tablespoons of sugar and seal. Like the peaches and pears and all preserves let them cool in the water in which they were sterilized and store in a dark place. I have discovered that leaving the pits in the plums and apricots makes them better with a taste a little like amaretto.

Put mulberries, raspberries, and figs into jars after having carefully washed them in water and lemon.

Fill the jars, add 3 tablespoons of sugar, and boil in cold water for 20 minutes.

★     ★     ★

## PEELED TOMATOES

Very simple: take ripe tomatoes, or better "plum" tomatoes, but you can also use the round tomatoes.

Put them in boiling water for 5 minutes, peel them, and leave them whole. Fill glass jars, putting fresh basil leaves and a pinch of salt over each layer so you'll have the minerals in the salt, which are very precious. Fill the jars well. Seal them and put them in cold water to boil for

20 minutes. Leave them in the water until they cool, otherwise, good-bye tomatoes!

**RAW TOMATO SAUCE**

Simple and very easy to use when ready.

Take ripe tomatoes, then prepare basil, parsley, and celery. Put the washed tomatoes, raw and with the skin, into the blender: cut the tomatoes into pieces and fill the blender halfway. Add a little basil, parsley, and celery.

Add a tablespoon of salt, blend for a minute, fill the jars, and seal. Put the jars in cold water and boil for 20 minutes. Let them cool and store them in a dark place. Use them for pasta, pizza, meat pizzaiola, baked macaroni, boiled rice, etc.

Make enough to last from December to July.

If you have the good fortune to have an apparatus called Bimby to prepare preserves, marmalade, fillings for stuffed peaches, stuffed zucchini, to keep frozen and to cook just before serving, it will be enjoyable. With Bimby, marmalade is made in a half hour by putting the ingredients in its pitcher.

By programming the speed and cooking time you can go about your business, Bimby will prepare your marmalade in a half hour without you. You'll also have tomato sauce and other sauces in 30 seconds and so on.

However, I am convinced that this should not be overdone. Prepare the things that you use, that your family likes. If you don't have a cool, dark place forget about making sauces because you will be disappointed when you dream of eating them. But if you prepare them well and have a place to store them, you'll save yourself work and have much satisfaction because you will offer good, wholesome, products made by you without preservatives.

## ROASTED, STUFFED PEPPERS

*Ingredients for 6 jars of peppers:*

**6½ lbs. yellow and red peppers**
**24 anchovies in salt**
    **olive oil, as much as needed**
**10½ oz. wine vinegar**

Wash and dry the peppers and roast them in a hot oven at 475° for 60 minutes.

When the peppers are well browned, take them out of the oven and . . . (try this trick!) put them in a plastic bag, immediately, while they are very hot. Close the bag and leave them there for a while.

In the meantime, clean the anchovies with paper towels, but don't rinse them! Open them, remove the bones, and prepare the fillets in a dish. Now open the plastic bag and peel the peppers.

You'll be able to do this easily because the water vapor formed in the bag will help the skin to peel from the peppers. Remove the seeds and divide the pepper into 8 pieces. When you have finished cutting the peppers, bring to a boil a saucepan with only the wine vinegar. When it boils throw in the peppers and return to a boil; boil for 3 minutes.

Drain the peppers, dry them with a cloth, and stuff each piece of pepper with an anchovy fillet. Roll it all up and put it in a low but wide glass jar. Cover with olive oil and store in the cellar.

It will seem troublesome and meticulous but it's necessary to boil the roasted peppers in the vinegar, otherwise you'll risk *fatal* food poisoning.

Many homemade preserves made without using common sense become poison. Botulism, the fungus that forms in homemade jars, dies in vinegar.

• Here's a winning antipasto!

★          ★          ★

## ANTIPASTO, PIEDMONT STYLE

*Ingredients for 10 jars, 7 oz. each:*

  2  **lbs. plum tomatoes**
10½  **oz. small onions**
10½  **oz. string beans**
10½  **oz. celery**
10½  **oz. carrots**
10½  **oz. peppers**
  1  **glass extra-virgin olive oil**
  1  **glass wine vinegar**
  1  **heaping tablespoon salt**
  1  **heaping tablespoon sugar**

Wash the tomatoes, cut them into pieces, put them in a pot, and cook without water. Add a little salt and cook, covered for 10 minutes. Put the tomatoes through a vegetable grinder and put the sauce in a large 7-quart pot.

Clean, wash, and cut into pieces all the indicated vegetables. Add them to the tomato sauce. Also add the oil, salt, and sugar and mix well.

Cook over low heat for 45 minutes from when it begins to boil. It's ready!

To preserve:

a) Put the product into the jars boiling hot, seal, cover, with a wool cloth, and let cool. Then label the jars with: "Antipasto, Piedmont Style," with the date of preparation. Store in a cool, dark place. It can be kept for 3-4 months.

b) Let the antipasto cool, then put it into jars, seal and sterilize (in cold water, boil for 20 minutes, turn off the heat and let it cool), and label it with the name and date. Store in a cool, dark place. You can keep it up to 12 months! It can be used as antipasto or as a side dish to pork steaks, meat, etc. Don't add preservatives, not even salicylic acid: it's against the 5th commandment!

*Note:* If you want the winter version you can substitute cauliflower for the string beans and artichokes for the peppers; the rest is the same as above.

# A SHORT GASTRONOMIC DICTIONARY

**Au Gratin** — To bake a pan of food topped with cheese, bread crumbs, or butter forming a light, golden crust.

**Bain-marie** (double-boiler) — The system of cooking food by which the receptacle containing the food is put over another one containing boiling water.

**Blend** — To mix together various ingredients until an homogeneous mixture is obtained.

**Boiling** — Said of a liquid, especially water, which reaches the temperature of 212° F (100° C) and is therefore, boiling.

**Braise** — To cook covered with very little water, generally in the oven.

**Bread Crumbs** — Can be made at home by grating dried leftover bread or can be bought ready made. They are used to bread foods in preparation for frying or in greased pans.

**Broth** — The liquid obtained by cooking beef, veal, or chicken with vegetables (celery, carrots, onions). Or more simply by melting a bouillon cube in the required amount of water.

**Clarify** — The process of making broth clearer. This is done by beating some egg whites and throwing them into the broth. As they solidify in the pot broth they absorb the excess fat and impurities. The broth is then strained.

**Cold** — Food at room temperature, not to be confused with frozen.

**Consistent** — Firm, thick, as pasta or meat slices 1-inch thick, or a sauce that doesn't drip from the spoon.

**Cooling** — Immersing a cooked food into cold water and draining. This procedure stops the cooking process.

**Croutons** — Small crisp pieces of toasted bread fried in butter or oil, used to garnish consomme or creamed soups.

**Cutting Board** — A wooden board on which to cut or chop food.

**Dilute**— To add liquid (water, broth, wine, milk, etc.) to a culinary preparation in a sufficient amount to give the proper consistency and to allow the continuation of the cooking process without the food sticking to the bottom.

**Dissolve** — To mix a substance with a liquid and blend well until there are no lumps.

**Entree** — A cold or hot course served fourth in important dinners, after soup or broth, fish, and meat.

**Fillets** — Long and narrow strips of meat cut from the breasts of chicken, turkey, and duck. The parts of a divided or split fish are also called fillets. In beef, veal, and pork the fillet is the part along the spinal column.

**Fruit Salad** — Made up of sliced fruit macerating in a syrup of brandy and lemon.

**Fry** — Method of cooking food by immersing it in boiling fat, which can be lard, oil, or butter. When using butter, a couple of spoonfuls of oil must be added to raise the temperature and make the food crispy.

**Giblets** — Liver, lungs, kidneys, heart, sweetbread, brains, tripe, veins of cattle and sheep, comb and entrails of poultry. The organ meats can be prepared in gravy and can be used to make a broth to add body to a sauce for chicken.

**Glaze** — To spoon a thick gravy over meat, or a thick sugar syrup over a dessert until a shiny crust is formed.

**Golden** ("Dorare") — To make a golden color; brushing the top of the dough with egg whites before cooking; breading and then frying food in butter or oil.

**Hard-boiled** — An egg cooked for 10 minutes in boiling water: the white and the yolk are solid.

**Line** — To cover the inside of a cooking pan or dish, whether it be with pasta or with slices of bacon.

**Macerate** To marinate fish or meat for some time in liquid (usually wine) seasoned with herbs and spices.

**Marinade** — The liquid used to marinate meat or fish.

**Mustard** — A sauce made basically with mustard seed and vinegar that can be bought prepared in jars. "Mostarda di Cremona" is a savory relish made of fruit preserved in a sweet syrup and flavored with mustard.

**"Pane Carre"** — White American bread already sliced. Used for toast, sandwiches, and croutons.

**Parboil** — To throw into boiling water for an instant. In the case of vegetables this allows for easy peeling of the skin. In the case of meat, to remove excess salt or to seal the external part so that internal juices don't escape.

**Pinch** — A very small quantity of condiment especially in powdered form (salt, pepper).

**Poach** — To cook in boiling water, especially eggs. To obtain good results, when the water boils lower the heat to minimum and only then break the egg into the water.

**Pound** — To make a piece of meat or fish thinner with a wooden mallet that makes the food more tender for cooking.

**Puree** — Mixture obtained from the prolonged cooking of food, which is then passed through a sieve.

**Reduce** — To diminish the volume of juice or sauce by cooking over high heat, uncovered so that it evaporates.

**Reviving** — Revive vegetables, legumes, or dried fruit by letting them soak in water.

**Sauté** — Cooking food in oil or butter over high heat, and turning it continuously so that it doesn't stick to the pan, until it becomes golden brown.

**Simmer** — To boil over very low heat, slowly.

**Skim** — Removing with a slotted spoon the foam formed when meats or legumes are boiled.

**Small bunch of Aromatic Herbs** — Used in many recipes. Can contain celery, parsley, laurel, thyme, and tarragon. They can be tied together with thin string or wrapped in gauze.

**Soak** — To soften an ingredient by putting it in water, wine, milk, or other liquids for the amount of time necessary for it to absorb the quantity wanted.

**"Soffritto"** — A sauce of minced onions fried in butter to which minced celery, parsley, and carrots can also be added.

**Spices** — Those substances (pepper, nutmeg, juniper, cloves, saffron, cinnamon, paprika, and others) that serve to flavor food.

**Steam** — To cook meat or vegetables in a covered pot allowing their juices to run out into the pot and without adding water or condiments.

**Stew** — To cook meat or vegetables over low heat in a covered pot with very little gravy.

**Strainer** — Kitchen utensil with a fine metal net.

**Stuffing** — Condiment composed of lard or bacon or prosciutto fat minced together with various herbs (celery, onions, carrots, parsley or marjoram, garlic) and fried.

**Stuff with Bacon** — To make the meat more tender and tastier by putting in pieces of lard or bacon, possibly flavored with aromatic herbs. The pieces of lard must be inserted in the same direction as the grain of the meat.

**Thicken Sauces** — For this operation butter, flour, cornstarch, eggs, or cream can be used. If flour or cornstarch are used mix them first with some butter to avoid lumps.

**To Bake in Foil** — A way to prepare fish or meat by wrapping it in aluminum foil so as to keep in the juices and seasonings and then baking in the oven.

**To Bread** — To dip food to be fried first in beaten eggs and then in bread crumbs.

**To Brown** — To put food in boiling oil to brown the exterior and seal in the juices.

**To Butter or Grease** — To spread butter on a pan that will go into the oven. It's better to use butter that has been taken out of the refrigerator a few minutes before and is, therefore, soft. Otherwise, melt it and brush it on.

**To Cream** — To beat while cooking a food to make it very smooth. Usually using cream, milk, or cheese.

**To Flambe** — To pass a chicken over a gas flame in order to remove any trace of fuzz or down. The term is also used in regard to a dessert in which rum or brandy is added and then ignited (flambe). To obtain good results the liqueur must be heated first.

**To Flavor** — Herbs or rinds are used to give flavor to foods.

**To Flour** — To sprinkle with flour or to dredge in flour. Sprinkle it on a pan so that the dough doesn't stick to it, or on meat after having let it set for a while to thicken the sauce. To fry fish, dip it first in milk and then in a plate full of flour.

**To Stuff** — To fill a chicken (or other foods) with a mixture, generally composed of bread crumbs, eggs, cheese, and aromatic herbs. This filling can also be called stuffing.

**Whip** — To beat eggs, cream, etc. with a fork or a whisk into a frothy, light composition increasing in volume.

**Whisk** — Kitchen utensil made of metal wires with a handle. It is used to whip eggs, egg whites, sauces, etc.

## Useful Information

| FOR 2 SERVINGS | RECEPTACLE | WATER | SALT |
|---|---|---|---|
| broth | 6″ saucepan | 2 cups | 1 tablespoon |
| soup | 12″ pot | 2 qts. | 2 tablespoons |
| pasta | 8″ pot | 1 qt. | 2 tablespoons |
| rice | 8″ saucepan | 2 cups | 2 tablespoons |
| potato gnocchi | 12″ pot | 2 qts. | 2 tablespoons |
| baked macaroni | 8″ baking pan | — | — |
| polenta | 8″ pot | 1 qt. | 1 tablespoon |
| roasted meat | 6″ pan | — | — |
| boiled meat | 8″ pot | 1 qt. | 2 tablespoons |
| stew | 6″ saucepan | — | 1 teaspoon |
| grilled steak | grill or griddle | — | 1 teaspoon |
| frankfurters | medium frying pan | — | — |
| baked fish | frying pan or oven on broil | — | as much as needed |
| boiled fish | 8″ fish kettle | 1 qt. | 2 tablespoons |
| fish stew | 6″ saucepan | — | 1 tablespoon |
| fish salad | salad bowl | — | 2 tablespoons |
| fried fish | medium frying pan | — | as much as needed |
| boiled vegetables | 6″ pot | 2 cups | 2 tablespoons |
| fried vegetables | medium frying pan | — | as much as needed |
| steamed vegetables | 6″ pan | — | 2 teaspoons |
| vegetable salad | salad bowl | — | 1 teaspoon |
| vegetable molds | 2 lb. baking pan | — | as much as needed |
| omelets | medium frying pan | — | as much as needed |
| gravies | medium saucepan | — | as much as needed |

# Useful Information

| CONDIMENTS | AMOUNT | COOKING TIME |
|---|---|---|
| butter or bouillon | 1½ oz. pasta | 15 minutes |
| butter - oil | 1½ oz. pasta | 2–3 hrs. |
| various sauces | 5¼ oz. pasta | 15 min. |
| butter - oil | 5¼ oz. rice | 15–20 min. |
| butter | 14 oz. | 3 min. |
| classic sauce | 7 oz. | 40 min. |
| 1 tablespoon oil | 7 oz. | 30 min. |
| oil - herbs | 14 oz. | 45–60 min. |
| various herbs | 17½ oz. meat | 60-80 min. |
| oil - herbs | 10½ oz. | 40–60 min. |
| — | 3½ oz. each | 4 min. |
| — | 14 oz. | 10 min. |
| a little oil - herbs | 10½-14 oz. | 15 min. |
| various herbs | 10½-14 oz. | varies |
| oil - herbs - tomato | 10½-14 oz. | 15 min. |
| oil - parsley - lemon | 10½-14 oz. | already cooked |
| olive oil | 7–10½ oz. | 8 min. |
| — | 10½ oz. | varies |
| olive oil | 10½ oz. | as much as needed |
| oil - butter - herbs | 10½ oz. | 30–40 min. |
| water or white wine - oil, vinegar - lemon | 7 oz. | already cooked or raw |
| butter - bread - white sauce | 14 oz. | 45-50 min. |
| oil - herbs | 2 eggs | 5 min. |
| oil - butter - herbs - chopped meat and sausage | 1 oz. each | 30-90 min. |

# EQUIPMENT NEEDED IN THE KITCHEN

Those who have a kitchen already equipped and in use need not read this short chapter. They already have everything they "truly need" or if they don't, they know what is missing and are planning to buy it. This is just a minimum guide for someone who truly has nothing and wants to buy the essential equipment needed to begin cooking.

## A Minimal List

In the table below are listed all the objects that seem indispensable to me, or almost indispensable, for every-day cooking for a family of about 3-5 persons.

Naturally, it is necessary to add to this all the objects needed to set the table and serve the food; dishes, flat-ware, salad bowl or tureen (except those which can also be used to cook), a couple of serving platters, a griddle, tea cups, and coffee cups.

You can erase from this minimal list anything that you don't foresee yourself using, but it is more probable that you will have to add items (for example, a cruet stand, a salt shaker, coasters, trivets, nutcrackers, etc.).

If, then, you pause to consider what would be conve-nient to have in the kitchen and what is available in the stores, the list would never end: new things are often found in stores that make everyday tasks as well as spe-cial tasks easier and faster.

- 3 frying pans of various sizes (about 8″, 10″ in diame-ter);

- 3 different sized pots (with 4″ high sides and about 6″, 7″, 8″ in diameter) with corre-sponding lids:

- a large pot for boiled meats, to cook and wash vegetables, to wash lettuce, to cook pasta or boil rice; with a corre-sponding cover;

- a colander;
- at least 1 pan for oven roasts;
- a 5-qt. pressure cooker;
- at least 2 knives, 1 large and 1 small; better yet, a few more at least of the small ones;

- forks and spoons to cook with, not expensive but of sturdy material; a few teaspoons;
- at least 1 wooden spoon, if possible 3, with different length handles or all long handles;
- a mixing spoon;
- a skimming spoon;
- 2 or 3 bowls of different sizes;
- plates, soup bowls, small plates, various bowls;
- a cheese grater or other utensils to grate cheese;
- a can opener;
- a bottle opener;
- a cutting board;
- a half moon knife or other utensil to chop herbs and other ingredients;
- a meat mallet;
- a funnel;
- at least 2 potholders;
- at least 4-6 dish towels;
- a knife sharpener;
- a coffee pot;
- a tea pot;
- small pot to heat milk, water for tea, etc.;
- a small strainer the right size for tea (but useful for other things as well) and if possible, another strainer 4 times larger than the first.

## APPROXIMATE WEIGHTS AND MEASURES

1 level tablespoon of flour = ⅓ oz.
1 level tablespoon of butter = ½ oz.
1 level tablespoon of sugar = ½ oz.
1 level tablespoon of oil = ½ oz.
1 level tablespoon of water = ½ oz.
1 level tablespoon of milk = ½ oz.
1 level tablespoon of semolina = ⅓ oz.
1 level tablespoon of cornstarch = ½ oz.
1 level tablespoon of tapioca = ½ oz.
1 level tablespoon of rice = ¾ oz.
1 level tablespoon of thin spaghetti (vermicelli) = ¾ oz.
1 level tablespoon of fine salt = ½ oz.
1 level tablespoon of gross salt = ¾ oz.
1 teaspoon of baking powder = .14 oz.
1 tea cup of almonds = 5 oz.
1 tea cup of raisins = 5¼ oz.
1 tea cup of bread crumbs = 1.7 oz.

# INDEX

### Fish